T0123486

MACAT

An Analysis of

Donna Haraway's

A Cyborg Manifesto: Science, Technology, and Socialist-Feminism in the Late Twentieth Century

Rebecca Pohl

Published by Macat International Ltd
24:13 Coda Centre, 189 Munster Road, London SW6 6AW.

Distributed exclusively by Routledge
2 Park Square, Milton Park, Abingdon, Oxon OX14 4RN
711 Third Avenue, New York, NY 10017, USA

Routledge is an imprint of the Taylor & Francis Group, an informa business

Copyright © 2018 by Macat International Ltd
Macat International has asserted its right under the Copyright, Designs and Patents Act
1988 to be identified as the copyright holder of this work.

The print publication is protected by copyright. Prior to any prohibited reproduction, storage in
a retrieval system, distribution or transmission in any form or by any means, electronic, me-
chanical, recording or otherwise, permission should be obtained from the publisher or where
applicable a license permitting restricted copying in the United Kingdom should be obtained
from the Copyright Licensing Agency Ltd, Barnard's Inn, 86 Fetter Lane, London EC4A 1EN, UK.

The ePublication is protected by copyright and must not be copied, reproduced, transferred,
distributed, leased, licensed or publicly performed or used in any way except as specifically
permitted in writing by the publishers, as allowed under the terms and conditions under which
it was purchased, or as strictly permitted by applicable copyright law. Any unauthorised distribution or use of this text may be a direct infringement of the authors and the publishers' rights
and those responsible may be liable in law accordingly.

www.macat.com
info@macat.com

Cataloguing in Publication Data
A catalogue record for this book is available from the British Library.
Library of Congress Cataloguing-in-Publication Data is available upon request.
Cover illustration: Etienne Gilfillan

ISBN 978-1-912453-56-6 (hardback)
ISBN 978-1-912453-11-5 (paperback)
ISBN 978-1-912453-26-9 (e-book)

Notice
The information in this book is designed to orientate readers of the work under analysis,
to elucidate and contextualise its key ideas and themes, and to aid in the development
of critical thinking skills. It is not meant to be used, nor should it be used, as a
substitute for original thinking or in place of original writing or research. References and
notes are provided for informational purposes and their presence does not constitute
endorsement of the information or opinions therein. This book is presented solely for
educational purposes. It is sold on the understanding that the publisher is not engaged
to provide any scholarly advice. The publisher has made every effort to ensure that
this book is accurate and up-to-date, but makes no warranties or representations with
regard to the completeness or reliability of the information it contains. The information
and the opinions provided herein are not guaranteed or warranted to produce particular
results and may not be suitable for students of every ability. The publisher shall not be
liable for any loss, damage or disruption arising from any errors or omissions, or from
the use of this book, including, but not limited to, special, incidental, consequential or
other damages caused, or alleged to have been caused, directly or indirectly, by the
information contained within.

CONTENTS

THE MACAT LIBRARY

The Macat Library is a series of unique academic explorations of seminal works in the humanities and social sciences – books and papers that have had a significant and widely recognised impact on their disciplines. It has been created to serve as much more than just a summary of what lies between the covers of a great book. It illuminates and explores the influences on, ideas of, and impact of that book. Our goal is to offer a learning resource that encourages critical thinking and fosters a better, deeper understanding of important ideas.

Each publication is divided into three Sections: Influences, Ideas, and Impact. Each Section has four Modules. These explore every important facet of the work, and the responses to it.

This Section-Module structure makes a Macat Library book easy to use, but it has another important feature. Because each Macat book is written to the same format, it is possible (and encouraged!) to cross-reference multiple Macat books along the same lines of inquiry or research. This allows the reader to open up interesting interdisciplinary pathways.

To further aid your reading, lists of glossary terms and people mentioned are included at the end of this book (these are indicated by an asterisk [*] throughout) – as well as a list of works cited.

Macat has worked with the University of Cambridge to identify the elements of critical thinking and understand the ways in which six different skills combine to enable effective thinking.
Three allow us to fully understand a problem; three more give us the tools to solve it. Together, these six skills make up the **PACIER** model of critical thinking. They are:

ANALYSIS – understanding how an argument is built
EVALUATION – exploring the strengths and weaknesses of an argument
INTERPRETATION – understanding issues of meaning

CREATIVE THINKING – coming up with new ideas and fresh connections
PROBLEM-SOLVING – producing strong solutions
REASONING – creating strong arguments

To find out more, visit **WWW.MACAT.COM.**

CRITICAL THINKING AND "A CYBORD MANIFESTO"

Primary critical thinking skill: INTERPRETATION
Secondary critical thinking skill: CREATIVE THINKING

Donna Haraway's work is known for its playful and sometimes challenging style as well as for its ability to yoke together an enormous variety of references from different fields. Part of the initial success of "A Cyborg Manifesto" was the audacity and creativity with which it was written, and this is what makes it a key work of creative thinking in the Macat library. However, we place this as the secondary critical thinking skill because Haraway's argument and ideas are not just a matter of new connections and novel explanations. In order to understand how she redefines the debates around feminism and technology, first it is essential to look carefully at the concepts, technical terms, and problems of definition in the manifesto and work through their meanings. Without this, we risk falling into some of the enthusiastic misreadings that so frustrated Haraway in the reception of her work.

Haraway's essay is itself an exercise in interpretation as well as creative thinking. As her earlier work on metaphor indicates, she is especially attuned to the meanings embedded in technical language, even the technical language of science (which is sometimes thought of as simply "plain" and not in need of interpretation). Haraway insists on the primary importance of interpretation, since this is part of the contest over the right to signify, which she sees at the heart of political struggle.

ABOUT THE AUTHOR OF THE "A CYBORD MANIFESTO"

Donna Haraway was born in Denver, Colorado in 1944. She trained as an experimental biologist but is best known for her work in cultural and feminist theory. Her most notable work is "A Cyborg Manifesto," first published in 1985 while she was working as a professor of feminist theory and technoscience at the University of California, Santa Cruz. Having been brought up a Catholic and becoming involved in the Catholic Left during her teenage years, she became increasingly involved in political activism through her time as a student at Colorado College, Yale University, and the Faculté de Sciences at the University of Paris on a Fulbright scholarship. She undertook doctoral research at Yale, beginning in experimental biology but then becoming more interested in the culture, politics, and language of science and technology, which would be the foundation of her research for the rest of her career. In addition to "A Cyborg Manifesto," Haraway has written books on metaphor in developmental biology (1976), primatology in the light of gender and race politics (1989), feminism and technoscience (1997), interspecies kinship (2003, 2008), and ecological catastrophe (2016).

ABOUT THE AUTHORS OF THE ANALYSIS

Rebecca Pohl is the co-editor of Rupert Thomson: Critical Essays (2016) and has published on contemporary women's writing, gender, and feminist theory. Her work in progress includes a manuscript that examines the impact of gender on mid-century experimental writing by women in Britain. She also regularly speaks at public events on the topics of gender and sexuality and women's writing. Pohl is Honorary Research Fellow in English Literature at the University of Manchester, an associate lecturer at Goldsmiths University London, and a contemporary literature supervisor at the University of Cambridge.

ABOUT MACAT

GREAT WORKS FOR CRITICAL THINKING

Macat is focused on making the ideas of the world's great thinkers accessible and comprehensible to everybody, everywhere, in ways that promote the development of enhanced critical thinking skills.

It works with leading academics from the world's top universities to produce new analyses that focus on the ideas and the impact of the most influential works ever written across a wide variety of academic disciplines. Each of the works that sit at the heart of its growing library is an enduring example of great thinking. But by setting them in context – and looking at the influences that shaped their authors, as well as the responses they provoked – Macat encourages readers to look at these classics and game-changers with fresh eyes. Readers learn to think, engage and challenge their ideas, rather than simply accepting them.

'Macat offers an amazing first-of-its-kind tool for interdisciplinary learning and research. Its focus on works that transformed their disciplines and its rigorous approach, drawing on the world's leading experts and educational institutions, opens up a world-class education to anyone.'

Andreas Schleicher,
Director for Education and Skills, Organisation for Economic
Co-operation and Development

'Macat is taking on some of the major challenges in university education ... They have drawn together a strong team of active academics who are producing teaching materials that are novel in the breadth of their approach.'

Prof Lord Broers,
former Vice-Chancellor of the University of Cambridge

'The Macat vision is exceptionally exciting. It focuses upon new modes of learning which analyse and explain seminal texts which have profoundly influenced world thinking and so social and economic development. It promotes the kind of critical thinking which is essential for any society and economy.
This is the learning of the future.'

Rt Hon Charles Clarke, former UK Secretary of State for Education

'The Macat analyses provide immediate access to the critical conversation surrounding the books that have shaped their respective discipline, which will make them an invaluable resource to all of those, students and teachers, working in the field.'

Professor William Tronzo, University of California at San Diego

WAYS IN TO THE TEXT

KEY POINTS

- Donna Haraway is a prominent feminist and cultural theorist best known for "A Cyborg Manifesto," first published in 1985.

- The manifesto presents the figure of the cyborg as an "ironic political myth" around which to build new possibilities for community and pleasure against the threat of domination and colonization.

- Haraway's essay is a seminal work in contemporary theory, partly because of its striking blend of disciplines, language, style, and register.

Who Is Donna Haraway?

Donna Haraway was born in Denver, Colorado, in 1944. She trained as an experimental biologist but is best known for her work in cultural and feminist theory. Her most notable work is "A Cyborg Manifesto: Science, Technology, and Socialist-Feminism* in the Late Twentieth Century," first published in 1985 while she was working as a professor of feminist theory and technoscience* at the University of California, Santa Cruz. Having been brought up a Catholic* and becoming involved in the Catholic Left* during her teenage years, she became increasingly involved in political activism through her time as a student at Colorado College, Yale University, and the Faculté de Sciences at the University of Paris 6 on a Fulbright* scholarship. She undertook doctoral research at Yale, beginning in experimental biology but then becoming more interested in the culture, politics, and language of science and technology, which would be the foundation of her research for the rest of her career. In addition to "A Cyborg Manifesto," Haraway has written books on metaphor in developmental biology (1976), primatology* in the light of gender and race politics (1989), feminism and technoscience (1997), interspecies kinship (2003, 2008), and ecological catastrophe (2016).

What Does "A Cyborg Manifesto" Say?

Cyborgs are not just figures of science fiction, Haraway argues, but representations of social reality. The cyborg, a hybrid of organism (human) and machine, reflects the ways in which developing technologies have pervaded the everyday lives of humans in an advanced industrial society like the United States: biotechnology,* medical advances, information and communications technology, mechanization of industry, and arms manufacture were all a prominent part of US-American culture and society in the 1980s.

Haraway paints a picture of the merging of technology, economics, and everyday life in the United States: Silicon Valley* had become recognized as a new center for entrepreneurial wealth and fast rates of profit, while the industries associated with these tech companies and multinationals were increasingly subject to offshoring*—moving factories overseas where workers could be paid lower wages and where new communications technologies and reductions in the time and cost of shipping made it possible to coordinate supply lines to the buying country. Meanwhile, the Strategic Defense Initiative,* otherwise known as the "Star Wars" program, promised to hand the United States dominance over the Soviet Union in a new arms race, which also included an $84 billion investment in C3I, or command-control-communication-intelligence. "Modern war," writes Haraway, "is a cyborg orgy, coded by C3I ... the military's symbol for its operations theory."[1] Command and control, supported by technologies of communication and intelligence (surveillance), seem to be increasingly dominant parts of social life, Haraway suggests. What's more, the mechanization of modern production makes it seem "like a dream of cyborg colonization work ... that makes the nightmare of Taylorism* seem idyllic."[2]

Haraway's depiction of contemporary America makes it seem like a technological nightmare, a dystopia* that has not yet quite revealed itself as a dystopia but keeps moving faster and faster in that direction. Cyborgs, then, are surely the figures that socialists,* feminists,* and other progressive or radical people need to oppose.

Far from it, says Haraway. "A Cyborg Manifesto" makes clear that there is no way of simply stepping outside of these conditions—no way of not being a cyborg, in Haraway's thinking. But being a cyborg does not have to mean being compliant, subservient to, or dominated by the prevailing economic and social conditions. Cyborgs, she writes, are "illegitimate offspring of militarism and patriarchal* capitalism, not to mention state socialism," and illegitimate offspring can be unruly and "are often exceedingly unfaithful to their origins."[3] Haraway then attempts to show the ways in which a synthesis of human and machine could produce new possibilities for coalition politics to resist the colonizing tendency as well as new possibilities for pleasure—sexual, intellectual—through the enhancement of bodily skill and the forging of different kinds of connection. The cyborg is therefore neither straightforwardly oppressive nor straightforwardly liberating, and the manifesto is calculated to expose and explore that tension.

Why Does "A Cyborg Manifesto" Matter?

"A Cyborg Manifesto" was originally published in the Socialist Review in 1985 (all citations are from this version of the text). Its full

11

original title gives a clear exposition of what it is about: "A Manifesto for Cyborgs: Science, Technology, and Socialist Feminism in the 1980s." It is a manifesto in the sense that it is calling for action, or activism, though the main call of the essay is for people to reshape their connections with one another and to reformulate their understanding of coalition and solidarity against oppressive and coercive power. Written in a highly energetic and playful but also rigorous and sometimes challenging style, it mixes registers, combines philosophy with popular culture and the language of contemporary high-tech science, and draws on a wide array of sources, from biologists to economists to philosophers, science fiction writers, and other feminist theorists. As a consequence, it is a work that has proven to be valuable and influential for people in a very wide variety of fields, not only in academia but also among activist communities and artists.

The manifesto was conceived as an intervention in debates about feminist theory and practice during the 1980s and especially as a critique of identity politics (feminism based on the idea of an essential, shared female identity) and humanism (the idea of an essential, shared human identity that distinguishes humans sharply from both animals and machines). Both of these types of critique have had a significant impact on the subsequent development of feminism and gender theory.*

NOTES

1   Donna Haraway, "A Manifesto for Cyborgs: Science, Technology, and Socialist Feminism in the 1980s," *Socialist Review*, 80 (1985), 65–107, 66.

2   Donna Haraway, "Manifesto," 66.

3   Donna Haraway, "Manifesto," 68.

SECTION 1
INFLUENCES

THE AUTHOR AND THE HISTORICAL CONTEXT

KEY POINTS

- "A Cyborg Manifesto" was a phenomenally successful and influential work of cultural theory.

- Donna Haraway's education and interests were strikingly interdisciplinary* and politically engaged.

- Haraway was keenly aware of being implicated in structures of oppression while also resisting them.

Why Read This Text?

"A Cyborg Manifesto: Science, Technology, and Socialist-Feminism in the Late Twentieth Century" is a seminal work in cultural theory that has impacted not only a number of academic disciplines, but also the political practice of many individuals and groups since its publication in 1985. In particular, the essay lays the groundwork for intersectional* perspectives on political theory and action. Intersectionality is an approach that considers the oppression and marginalization of certain groups (based on characteristics such as race, disability, sex, class, and sexual orientation) as inseparably connected and insists on understanding and counteracting them in relation to one another, rather than isolating and prioritizing one group. It rejects singularity and concentrates on overlapping forms of oppression.

The relevance of the manifesto to contemporary political debates has partly to do with the fact that Haraway engages with the complex interactions between race, sex, class, and sexuality in the context of an accelerating relationship between machine technology and people's everyday lived experience. The growth of the internet, social media,

> ❝ I am conscious of the odd perspective provided by my historical position—a PhD in biology for an Irish Catholic girl was made possible by Sputnik's* impact on US national science-education policy. I have a body and mind as much constructed by the post-Second World War arms race and Cold War as by the women's movements. ❞
>
> Donna Haraway, "A Cyborg Manifesto"

and the digital economy* has continued and exacerbated these trends, which contributes to the manifesto's ongoing significance. In some respects, "A Cyborg Manifesto" is of its era: the specific conditions of the 1980s and the prevalent ideas of postmodernism* or postmodernity. However, some of the problems and criticisms that it outlines have persisted and been further explored by other writers, and the essay is important in understanding some of the developments in contemporary critical theory.

Author's Life

Donna Haraway was born in 1944 in Denver, Colorado. Her father worked as a sportswriter for the Denver Post and walked with crutches for most of his life due to childhood tuberculosis. Haraway shared with him an enjoyment of sport and of words. Her mother came from a working-class Irish-Catholic background. Haraway went to the same convent school as her mother and was a committed Catholic in her childhood, though even early on she had doubts about this faith. Nevertheless, it was part of her political formation, since she became a member of the Catholic Left in high school. Her political activism at this time "meant for [her] a religiously motivated Catholic activism." [1] Despite later moving away from Catholicism, this activist strain remained significant for Haraway.

After high school, Haraway received a scholarship to study at Colorado College. Her majors were in zoology, philosophy, and literature. She also studied philosophy and theology in Paris on a Fulbright scholarship after her first degree before undertaking doctoral study in biology at Yale University. Although at first Haraway was conducting experimental biological research, she found herself more and more interested in the history, philosophy, culture, and politics of biology.

During the late 1960s, Haraway became more politically active in the anti-war movement and lived in an activist commune in New Haven, Connecticut. There she met Jaye Miller, a PhD student in history; they became friends, lovers, and married in 1970. Miller was gay, but only just coming out, and he and Haraway were both involved in gay liberation activism. This continued when they both moved to Honolulu, teaching at the University of Hawaii. Ultimately they divorced, but stayed very close.

Haraway completed her dissertation while working in Hawaii and received her doctorate in 1972. In 1974, she took a job as assistant professor in the Department of the History of Science at Johns Hopkins University in Baltimore, Maryland. In 1980, she was appointed to a tenure-track professorship in the History of Consciousness Department at the University of California, Santa Cruz (UCSC). The job was the first in the United States explicitly dedicated to feminist theory.[2] She was tenured in 1984, and "A Cyborg Manifesto" was published the following year.

At Johns Hopkins, Haraway met and began a relationship with Rusten Hogness; they have lived together since that point. In 1977, Haraway and Hogness, together with Miller and his friend Nick Paulina, bought land in Healdsburg, a small town in northern California. They lived in a community household together, and according to one former graduate student at UCSC, "live[d] the theory" Haraway wrote and taught. She goes on: "I saw it as this kind of utopian unit […] all of you forging your own kind of particular bonds." Haraway describes the "Manifesto" as being "in the utopian tradition," though she later insisted that this does not mean a "utopian dream but an on-the-ground working project."[3]

Author's Background

Haraway describes herself as having learned to read and write "inside worlds at war": she was born towards the end of the Second World War, her education took place in the years of the Cold War, and her formative years in graduate school coincided with the Vietnam War.[4] The anti-war movement of the late 1960s is a crucial background for her work in general; in turn, "A Cyborg Manifesto" was written in the mid-1980s during a phase of increasing militarism in the United States. Part of its immediate context is the so-called Reagan Doctrine,* which included an attempt to reject "Vietnam Syndrome"* (a widespread public dislike of overseas military action following the Vietnam War) and cultivate support for US involvement in violent conflict, sometimes through support for foreign fighters, and sometimes through direct action. There was also a renewed investment by the US in armaments and military technology—a high-tech arms race that the text also recognizes.

In the "Manifesto," Haraway alludes in a number of places to Silicon Valley as a central location (or "protoype") for the kind of technological developments she describes and critiques.[5] In the 1980s, Silicon Valley was becoming more prominent as a center for the development of information and communication technologies and for the entrepreneurial production of wealth. It was viewed as a nexus of technology and capitalism.

Haraway mentions the Livermore Action Group (LAG), an anti-nuclear activist group based in California that engaged in civil disobedience and nonviolent direct action. Just as anti-war activism was part of Haraway's intellectual formation, anti-nuclear activism—and especially the types of community and network that engaged in it—were part of the immediate background of the manifesto. More broadly, the text speaks to a wide range of Left*—liberal activist movements of the 1980s: feminist, environmentalist, anti-nuclear, socialist, and gay rights. These were significant but marginal movements struggling in relation to the dominant economic and social forces of the decade. Haraway herself has noted that she began to write the text "in the context of the early Reagan* era and the retrenchment of the Left that the 1980s was witnessing." She was responding to a call for essays about the future of socialist feminism from the journal Socialist Review.

NOTES

1   Donna Haraway and Thyrza Goodeve, *How Like a Leaf: An Interview with Donna Haraway* (New York: Routledge, 2000), 13.

2   Haraway and Goodeve, *How Like a Leaf*, 37.

3   Haraway and Goodeve, *How Like a Leaf*, 63.

4   Nick Gane and Donna Haraway, "When We Have Never Been Human, What Is to Be Done? Interview with Donna Haraway," *Theory, Culture & Society* 23 (2006), 135–58.

5   Haraway, "A Manifesto for Cyborgs: Science, Technology, and Socialist Feminism in the 1980s," *Socialist Review*, 80 (1985), 86.

6   Donna Haraway, Nina Lykke, Randi Markussen, and Finn Olesen, "Cyborgs, coyotes, and dogs: a kinship of feminist figurations" and "There are always more things going on than you thought! Methodologies as thinking technologies," in *The Haraway Reader* (New York: Routledge, 2004), 321–42, 323.

ACADEMIC CONTEXT

KEY POINTS

- Donna Haraway's interdisciplinary essay was written at the height of the feminist sex wars.*

- She seeks to distinguish her approach through a difference in tone and an intersectional perspective.

- Principal influences on the essay include her graduate students, black feminists, science fiction writers, and poststructuralist theorists.

The Work in Its Context

Donna Haraway's "A Cyborg Manifesto: Science, Technology, and Socialist-Feminism in the Late Twentieth Century" is very much an interdisciplinary work, both in its composition and its influence. For our purposes, the primary disciplinary background to look at will be feminist cultural theory—more specifically, in Haraway's own words at the start of the manifesto, socialist-feminism. It is important to note, however, that the purpose of the manifesto is partly to critique the application of sharp disciplinary boundaries and to focus instead on intersections between them.

Haraway also self-consciously positions the manifesto as a response to the "Western" traditions of science and politics, which means that it is meant to speak to trans-disciplinary structures of thinking. In particular, Haraway responds to three "boundary breakdowns" (collapsed dualisms*): she argues that the boundaries between animal/human, organism/machine, and physical/non-physical are no longer firm.[1] In this respect, the text also comes out of an engagement with post-structuralist* theory. Notably, Haraway discusses the concept of phallogocentrism*—the structure of thought and language that

> ❝ With the hard-won recognition of their social and historical constitution, gender, race, and class cannot provide the basis for belief in 'essential' unity. There is nothing about being 'female' that naturally binds women ... Gender, race, or class consciousness is an achievement forced on us by the terrible historical experience of the contradictory social realities of patriarchy, colonialism, and capitalism. ❞
>
> Donna Haraway, "A Cyborg Manifesto"

reinforces male dominance—citing Jacques Derrida* and Luce Irigaray* in particular. She is interested in "releasing the play of writing": breaking with the idea of language or concepts having fixed, pure, essential or "original" meaning, which post-structuralist feminists like Irigaray had associated with patriarchal domination.

In relation to feminist theory, Haraway was writing in the context of what is commonly called second-wave feminism*: a systematic questioning and critique of established gender roles emerging out of the women's rights and women's liberation movements. By the mid-1980s, major divisions had developed in these movements, notably in the US around the so-called feminist sex wars—debates about what constituted a "proper" feminist attitude towards sexuality and the body.

The 1980s also saw a significant expansion of cultural studies* as an academic discipline in US-American universities. Cultural studies developed at the University of Birmingham in England, and many of the scholars associated with it had roots in Marxist* and socialist theory. Broadly, it was devised as a discipline with a non-restrictive focus on cultural practices (which might include television, film, shopping, or the fashion tastes of a particular subculture) that would seek to analyze these practices in relation to wider power structures. The non-restrictive, often intersectional focus of cultural studies has affinities with Haraway's approach in the manifesto.

Overview of the Field

First of all, Haraway responds to the prevailing tone of socialist-feminist cultural theory, which she sees as being one of earnest, serious, reverent commitment. Against this, the manifesto will adopt a tone of irony and "blasphemy."[2] Relatively early in the essay, she focuses her critique of contemporary feminism on Catherine MacKinnon,* who had become well known for campaigning against pornography and sexual assault. The significance of MacKinnon's work in feminist theory was to argue that female experience—parallel to working class experience in Marxism—is defined by being deprived of one's sexuality. Haraway regards MacKinnon's theory as totalizing and restrictive. Instead, she advocates a different perspective on feminism that was emerging in the 1980s: understanding and criticizing "women's dominations of each other" along race or class lines, even within the feminist movement.[3] More sympathetically, Haraway critiques radical feminists such as Audre Lorde,* Adrienne Rich,* and Susan Griffin* for a too-restrictive focus on the "organic" as opposed to the "technological." Haraway will argue that this opposition no longer holds.

In parallel to this, Haraway takes issue with critiques of capitalist modernity that seem to advocate a "domination of technics" by an "imagined organic body" such as Herbert Marcuse's* One-Dimensional Man and Carolyn Merchant's* *Death of Nature.*[4] She notes the staunch feminist and Marxist critiques of post-structuralist theory. These critiques responded to the post-structuralist insistence that every structure and object of knowledge was a kind of text—il n'y a de hors-texte (there is no outside-the-text), in Jacques Derrida's famous expression—by arguing that this perspective leaves no room for understanding the real, lived, physical, and material relations between people and institutions.

Haraway cites Fredric Jameson's* work on postmodernism approvingly. For her, Jameson was right to suggest that "one cannot be for or against post-modernism," which she regards as "an essentially moralist move." Instead, postmodernism should be understood as a name for the inescapable social conditions that structure contemporary lived experience. She cites Michel Foucault's* work but notes that he was describing a form of power "at its moment of implosion." Instead of being dominated by "medicalization and normalization" (as in Foucault), we are now dominated by "networking, communications redesign, stress management."[5] Haraway does not fully elaborate on the difference between these forms of domination, but the implicit difference is between unifying or reductive methods (like organizing a whole range of different symptoms under a single medical diagnosis, such as hysteria) and methods which multiply connections to the point that they shape our lives without being within our control (like the information gathered and manipulated from social media). The "Cyborg Manifesto" is a response to these problems in cultural theory.

Academic Influences

Haraway's writing is very distinctive, and the style and argument of the manifesto suggest a very confident critical approach that may synthesize a variety of different influences but does not directly follow in any particular scholar's footsteps. Notably, she cites a number of doctoral dissertations and PhD-qualifying essays from UCSC, as well as an unpublished work on stress by her partner Rusten Hogness, which is "available from the author" (she includes a correspondence address); her "influences" are not necessarily prestigious academic figures but seem to be rooted in the practice and communities of teaching.[6] The particular nature of UCSC's degree programs in the History of Consciousness, as discussed in Module 7, alongside its faculty members and their keen engagement with postmodern and post-structuralist theory, also helped to shape the manifesto.

Haraway's critique of totalizing and identity-based feminist theory is influenced by the work of black feminists such as Bernice Reagon* and bell hooks,* arguing for coalition within the feminist movement based on affinity rather than identity. Nancy Hartsock* is cited prominently for her publications on feminism and materialism, including her notion of a "feminist standpoint" as a foundation for cultural theory. Haraway also makes a point of thanking her for their friendship and discussion in the essay's acknowledgements. Besides this, Haraway identifies a number of science-fiction writers as formative for the work: Samuel Delaney,* James Tiptree Jr.,* Vonda MacIntryre,* and Octavia Butler,* in particular.

NOTES

1   Haraway, "A Manifesto for Cyborgs: Science, Technology, and Socialist Feminism in the 1980s," *Socialist Review*, 80 (1985), 68.

2   Haraway, "Manifesto," 65.

3   Haraway, "Manifesto," 73.

4   Haraway, "Manifesto," 71.

5   Haraway, "Manifesto," 69n.

6   Haraway, "Manifesto," 16n, 104.

MODULE 3
THE PROBLEM

KEY POINTS

- Donna Haraway asks how socialist-feminism can organize itself to oppose the dominant social order.

- Haraway's interlocutors in the essay are not only established academics, but doctoral students as well as prominent postmodernist and post-structuralist thinkers.

- She is sharply critical of identity-based feminist politics, arguing instead for solidarity based on coalition and kinship.

Core Question

Given the fast-changing material circumstances of work, communication, and lived experience in a late-twentieth-century capitalist economy (specifically in the United States), as well as the developments in biotechnology, information technology, and arms manufacture that were part of public consciousness in the 1980s, and given the fragmentation of the feminist movement and of socialist politics, as well as the electoral success and ideological dominance of free-market capitalism, social conservatism, and resurgent militarism in this period, how can socialist-feminism organize itself to oppose and hopefully change the dominant social order?

This is the question Donna Haraway asks in "A Cyborg Manifesto: Science, Technology, and Socialist-Feminism in the Late Twentieth Century," and it is clearly about practical politics as much as academic debate. Nevertheless, the core question that the manifesto poses is theoretical: how can individual subjects recognize their own status and the conditions that dominate and shape them, and how can they recognize themselves as part of a group or coalition that could effectively oppose these conditions? This means that the manifesto

> **❝** Who are my kin in this odd world of promising monsters, vampires, surrogates, living tools, and aliens? How are natural kinds identified in the realms of late-twentieth-century technoscience? What kinds of crosses and offspring count as legitimate and illegitimate, to whom and at what cost? Who are my familiars, my siblings, and what kind of livable world are we trying to build? **❞**
>
> Donna Haraway, "FemaleMan©_Meets_OncoMouse"

can be contextualized in relation to theories of class consciousness. In the 1980s, the debates around this topic usually focused on a loss of group identity, partly as a consequence of deindustrialization.* But the manifesto should also be contextualized in relation to theories of feminist collective action. In the 1980s, these debates usually focused on the fragmentation of women's movements through either a loss of collective identity or too narrow a definition of female identity.

In both cases, the issue at stake had to do with definitions of identity. Haraway responds to this with a critique of the focus on identity itself. In doing so, she builds on contemporary criticisms about the way in which women of color had been dominated and marginalized within the feminist movement and the way in which anti-colonial standpoints had been—unintentionally, for the most part, but sometimes purposely—erased. This is similar to the feminist critique of socialist theories which treated class as the most fundamental form of group identity, relegating female experience to either a subset or—at worst—a distraction from class struggle. Likewise, Haraway takes issue with feminist theories that treat female identity as the center and any consideration of race, class, or colonialism as incidental.

The Participants

Haraway cites a great number of writers in the manifesto, engaging directly with some of them and contextualizing her argument with the others. Not all of the participants in the debate were well-established academic figures; Haraway discusses at length the doctoral work of students at UCSC, for example. Equally, she responds to the work of more prominent feminist, Marxist, and post-structuralist critics.

The work of Barbara Smith,* Bernice Reagon, bell hooks, Chela Sandoval,* and Katie King* is particularly significant in connection with the affirmation of "affinity, not identity" and of a unity "through coalition."[1] Haraway juxtaposes them to the feminist theory of Catherine MacKinnon, which operates according to a principle of identity between women based on their shared experience of dispossession. Haraway sees a similar problem in some Marxist theory, such as Herbert Marcuse's *One-Dimensional Man*, which in her view positions the human body (focusing on its desires and drives) as a similar principle of identity.

The manifesto is informed by post-structuralist and postmodern theory, although mostly as a background for Haraway's specific arguments about feminism and race: she cites Jacques Derrida, Claude Lévi-Strauss,* Luce Irigaray, and Monique Wittig* to highlight their critique of Western phallogocentrism, but departs from them to focus on US-American women of color and questions "about access to the power to signify."[2] Jean Baudrillard's* theory of the simulacrum*—a copy with no original—contextualizes her description of the technological landscape of the 1980s. Fredric Jameson's theory of postmodernism as a dominant cultural formation and a structure of lived experience (as opposed to a mere style, or a type of taste) also appears in Haraway's analysis.

The Contemporary Debate

Reagon's "Coalition Politics, Turning the Century" is a significant essay in Haraway's attempt to articulate a politics of affiliation rather than identity. Based on a presentation given at the West Coast

Women's Music Festival of 1981, Reagon's essay argues that "you shouldn't look for comfort" in a coalition; rather than trying to find "a bottle with some milk in it," or "a home" (which Haraway transposes into a desire for identification), Reagon insists that in a coalition, "you have to give" and that "you can't stay there all the time."[3] She argues that the women's movement has held to a view that there is an essential common experience between women, and this, she says, is a myth.

Sandoval's essay, "US Third World Feminism: The Theory and Method of Oppositional Consciousness in the Postmodern World" on "oppositional consciousness"* examines the ways in which categories of identity politics (for example, the "woman" in the women's movement) tend to be based on exclusions (for example, of nonwhite women).[4] She argues that instead of basing collective action on the idea that all women share some essential, natural characteristic, feminist activism could be based on coalition, affinity, and kinship. King's dissertation critiques the categories that had come to be used habitually to define different types of feminism (radical, liberal, and socialist), arguing that this approach tends to either incorporate or marginalize feminist practices that deviate from them.[5]

Haraway's major critique is of MacKinnon's article, "Feminism, Marxism, Method, and the State." For MacKinnon, patriarchal society involves the "organized expropriation of the sexuality of some for the use of others," and this is what defines and controls women's experience.[6] Haraway and others were sharply critical of MacKinnon's argument, partly because it tended to exclude internal difference and partly because, as Haraway points out, defining women in this way means that they are completely defined by reference to the desire of someone else—in this case, men in general.[7]

NOTES

1   Haraway, "A Manifesto for Cyborgs: Science, Technology, and Socialist Feminism in the 1980s," *Socialist Review*, 80 (1985), 73.

2   Haraway, "Manifesto," 93.

3   Bernice Johnson Reagon, "Coalition Politics: Turning the Century," in *Home Girls: A Black Feminist Anthology*, ed. Barbara Smith (New York: Kitchen Table: Women of Color Press, 1983), 356–68, 359.

4   Chela Sandoval, "U.S. Third World Feminism: The Theory and Method of Oppositional Consciousness in the Postmodern World," *Genders*, 10 (1991), 1–24.

5   Haraway, "Manifesto," 73–4.

6   Catherine A. MacKinnon, "Feminism, Marxism, Method, and the State: An Agenda for Theory," *Signs*, 7.3 (1982), 515–44, 516.

7   Haraway, "Manifesto," 77.

THE AUTHOR'S CONTRIBUTION

KEY POINTS

- "A Cyborg Manifesto" aims to present a "myth" that affords a new perspective on the relationship between animals, humans, and technology.

- The key philosophical point is about a perceived breakdown of boundaries and dualisms in a postmodern, technologically advanced society.

- Anti-colonial feminist theory is a key inspiration for Donna Haraway, who seeks a more inclusive idea of feminism.

Author's Aims

The first distinctive aim of Donna Haraway's essay "A Cyborg Manifesto: Science, Technology, and Socialist-Feminism in the Late Twentieth Century" is to change the tone of academic debate from one of earnest seriousness and faithful commitment to one of irony and blasphemy. For her, using an ironic tone serves to preserve contradictions, avoiding the attempt to dominate or incorporate differences that she thinks is characteristic of other feminist and socialist arguments. Rather than resolving contradictions into "larger wholes" (for example, suggesting that whatever differences of race, class, or disability individuals have, they should be united under a higher concept, such as female identity), Haraway claims that irony is about "the tension of holding incompatible things together because both or all are necessary and true."[1] The blasphemous tone is aimed at remaining faithful to community and collective action (not rejecting feminism or socialism) but avoiding the self-righteous moralism that also leads to exclusion and domination. Perhaps playing on the

> ❝ This is a dream not of a common language, but of a powerful infidel heteroglossia★... It means both building and destroying machines, identities, categories, relationships, space stories. Though both are bound in the spiral dance, I would rather be a cyborg than a goddess ❞
>
> Donna Haraway, "A Cyborg Manifesto"

language of her own Catholic background, Haraway distinguishes between blasphemy (which stays attached to the faith but is critical and irreverent about it) and apostasy (which renounces the faith entirely). In this case, the faith is to the feminist movement: political rather than religious.

Haraway's second goal is to use her specific knowledge of biology and biotechnology to inform a new perspective on the relationship between animals, humans, and technology, offering a new way of thinking about pleasure, responsibility, and unity between people trying to resist domination.

The third significant aim of the manifesto is to present a "myth" (the myth of the cyborg) that should be viewed from two contradictory perspectives: the cyborg as a symbol of absolute control, the imposition of technological domination on human existence; and the cyborg as a symbol of fearless and pleasurable kinship between animals, humans, and machines. For Haraway, it is crucial to keep both of these contradictory perspectives in mind rather than deciding for one side or the other.

Approach

Haraway's approach in this essay is partly suggested by the title she gave to the original essay: "A Manifesto for Cyborgs: Science, Technology, and Socialist Feminism in the 1980s." Calling it a "manifesto" and addressing her audience as cyborgs ("we are cyborgs," she says explicitly) is part of the ironic and blasphemous tone she seeks to convey, playing with and stretching some of the conventions of academic writing. At the same time, the essay is thoroughly academic, assembling a very wide range of sources to substantiate and prompt her arguments.

The main philosophical underpinning of Haraway's argument is her sense of collapsed dualisms or boundary breakdowns between animal/human, organism/machine, and physical/non-physical. Crucially, she does not suggest that this is straightforwardly good or bad. Instead, she regards it as a "cultural dominant," a condition of people's experience in the late twentieth century that needs to be recognized in order for "progressive people" to understand themselves and fight for their own freedom.[2]

This approach allows Haraway to use the cyborg as a "mythical" figure and explore its significance. Together with her immersion in biology, biotechnology, socialist-feminist theory, and the philosophy of knowledge (epistemology*), Haraway's approach to the question focuses on popular culture. The cyborg is, in some respects, a philosophical figure for her, but it is also a type of character that appears in science fiction books and films.

Contribution in Context

Perhaps the most important context for Haraway's distinctive political argument is anti-colonial and post-colonial perspectives on feminism, such as those that were being advanced by other feminist writers including bell hooks, Bernice Reagon, Barbara Smith, and Chela Sandoval. Haraway adopts ideas of coalition and kinship (as opposed to identity and essence) from these writers. She also recognizes and builds on Edward Said's* critique of orientalism: the false and fetishized ideas of non-Western people and culture that European scientists, artists, and writers produced as part of the colonial project.

The philosophical underpinnings of Haraway's argument build on ideas that were, by 1985, quite familiar from postmodern and post-structuralist theory. The idea of collapsed dualisms or boundary breakdowns between concepts (animal/human, organism/technology, nature/culture) is central to deconstructionist thought, most closely associated with Jacques Derrida. Haraway cites Derrida, as well as the structuralist anthropologist Claude Lévi-Strauss, whose work also called Western philosophical dualisms into question.

Haraway is sympathetic to some of the criticisms that had been made of poststructuralist thinking by socialist and feminist thinkers (above all, that it reduces human activity to a mere "play" of language); however, she sees the breakdown in dualisms as a real condition of people's experience in the 1980s—agreeing with Fredric Jameson on this—and so for her, the question is more about how to recognize and respond to these circumstances.

NOTES

1 Haraway, "A Manifesto for Cyborgs: Science, Technology, and Socialist Feminism in the 1980s," *Socialist Review*, 80 (1985), 65.

2 Haraway, "Manifesto," 71.

SECTION 2
IDEAS

MAIN IDEAS

KEY POINTS

- "A Cyborg Manifesto" insists that we are all cyborgs already, and that the question is how to contest what that means.

- Cyborgs are incorporated into networks of command and control, but they also have a tendency to rebel.

- Donna Haraway synthesizes a blend of vocabularies, registers, and styles that can be both challenging and playful to read—and is a crucial part of her argument.

Key Themes

Donna Haraway outlines her aim very clearly in the opening sentence of "A Cyborg Manifesto: Science, Technology, and Socialist-Feminism in the Late Twentieth Century": "to build an ironic political myth faithful to feminism, socialism, and materialism." Haraway's central idea is that the cyborg, a figure familiar from science fiction but in her view also a "creature of social reality," can be used to represent that myth.[1] The first main idea is that the cyborg is not just a creature of science fiction. Changes in technology and culture in the late twentieth century mean that we are cyborgs: modern medicine involves couplings between humans and machines; modern production processes and modern warfare both involve a fusion (or confusion) of man and machine.

From one perspective, all this sounds like something that must be resisted. It suggests that people are increasingly dominated by abstract forces and the intrusion of technology on their lives from corporations, the military, and the state. But Haraway thinks that there is potential

> ❝ The main trouble with cyborgs, of course, is that they are the illegitimate offspring of militarism and patriarchal capitalism, not to mention state socialism. But illegitimate offspring are often exceedingly unfaithful to their origins. Their fathers, after all, are inessential. ❞
>
> Donna Haraway, "A Cyborg Manifesto"

for both resistance (opposition) and pleasure (building something new) in accepting the nature of the cyborg. Specifically, because the cyborg is based on a breakdown of firm divisions between organisms and machines, it can symbolize relationships based not on identity but on coalition.

The feminist theory that argues all women should work together with each other because they share an identity as women, according to Haraway, has always tended to marginalize and exclude certain types of women (for example, women of color). Furthermore, the new material circumstances of work in the late twentieth century mean that many of the old, established "identities" (around class, gender, and race) have been dismantled. A better foundation, she argues, would be to accept yourself as a "cyborg"—already mixed up in biology and technology—but to contest what that will mean.

Exploring the Ideas

Changes in technology have been inseparable from changes in the nature of the economy, work, and everyday life, Haraway argues. The mixing of human and machine that creates the image of the cyborg in science fiction is not just imaginary, she says, but real: such hybrids are an essential characteristic of the global economy developing through the 1980s, from microelectronics to communications technologies to immunobiology and molecular genetics. These changes are drastic and all-pervasive. Notably, they completely change the types of employment available and consequently shift the power dynamics among different groups. Haraway sees the new technologies as contributing factors in this, particularly communication technologies, which allow labor forces and supply lines to be coordinated and controlled despite them being geographically distant. Outsourcing* and mechanization mean that workers who had previously been able to organize and exert enough pressure to maintain some job security and reasonable working conditions (unions and the "traditional" working class, predominantly white males) have become increasingly vulnerable to redundancy.

Haraway refers to this as a "feminization" of labor, because the precariousness and disenfranchisement now being experienced by these workers were already the dominant conditions for women's work. She argues that the place of women in these new working conditions has also changed, intensifying insecurity and demanding an urgent political (activist) response. Not only are women employed more and more often as the exploited workforce, but new demands are being made on them as caregivers and providers because of the erosion of welfare support. Haraway also points out that black women in the United States were already familiar with such "feminization" of work. Her point is to encourage her readers to recognize differential inequalities—specific differences in people's experience, and especially in their degree of disenfranchisement. She writes: "It is crucial to remember that what is lost, perhaps especially from women's points of view, is often virulent forms of oppression."[2] But this is meant to motivate a search for new kinds of coalition as part of a "progressive" or socialist-feminist politics.

How do cyborgs fit into this? First of all, transformations in technology and the fusion or confusion of humans and machines are part of the oppressive conditions Haraway describes—from military hardware to home entertainment, communication technology, and video games, human melding with technology is part of a widespread loss of skills, literacy, and autonomy. However, there is potential for another side to the story, Haraway argues; by "embracing the possibilities inherent in the breakdown of clean distinctions between organism and machine," it might be possible for feminists to reorganize and to "subvert command and control" in new ways.[3] These breakdowns create new possibilities for relationships of resistance, support, and pleasure, she argues. Ultimately, cyborgs (that is, all of us) are "the illegitimate offspring of militarism and patriarchal capitalism." We cannot get away from being their offspring—that is, our selves and experiences are unavoidably shaped by them—but "illegitimate offspring are often exceedingly unfaithful to their origins."[4] Cyborgs, in other words, have a tendency to rebel.

Language and Expression

The manifesto is challenging to read, but not written in a particularly "difficult" style compared to some other critical theory from the same period. In order to understand Haraway's arguments, it does help to have a working knowledge of some philosophical, political, and scientific language. The primary readership for the text when Haraway first published it was probably people already engaged in feminist theory and politics and who would have been at least somewhat versed in the current debates and the language of those debates. For example, the difference between "radical feminism"* and "socialist feminism" is important to understanding the text, although it is possible to infer the differences just by reading carefully.

Haraway's stated intention to write an "ironic" and "blasphemous" political myth partly influences the style of the text, as does the fact that she is (according to the title, at least) writing a "manifesto." She appeals to the reader quite often with collective pronouns, moves between tones (from serious polemic to sharp irony), and uses some memorable, aphoristic turns of phrase: "Our machines are disturbingly lively, and we ourselves frighteningly inert."[6]

What is perhaps most striking and influential about Haraway's language is that it synthesizes the vocabulary of philosophy (dualism, ontology,* teleology*), feminist practice (coalition, patriarchy, reproductive politics), and contemporary technology (integrated circuit, genetic engineering, immunobiology) together with a wide-ranging discussion of both economic structures and cultural practices, and a persistent focus on the language of race and anti-colonialism. This mix of discourses is perhaps part of what Haraway means at the end of the manifesto, where she writes of "a dream … of a powerful infidel heteroglossia" (heteroglossia meaning many tongues) rather than a "common language."[6]

NOTES

1   Haraway, "A Manifesto for Cyborgs: Science, Technology, and Socialist Feminism in the 1980s," Socialist Review, 80 (1985), 65.

2   Haraway, "Manifesto," 91.

3   Haraway, "Manifesto," 92.

4   Haraway, "Manifesto," 68.

5   Haraway, "Manifesto," 69.

6   Haraway, "Manifesto," 101.

MODULE 6
SECONDARY IDEAS

KEY POINTS

- The new possibilities of pleasure afforded by cyborg blending of human and technology are just as important as the need for collective action.

- Literacy of various kinds is a crucial part of political potential, as well as another potential source of pleasure.

- Donna Haraway's practice of citation in "A Cyborg Manifesto" seem to reflect her political commitments.

Other Ideas

If Donna Haraway's central point in "A Cyborg Manifesto: Science, Technology, and Socialist-Feminism in the Late Twentieth Century" is to show that there is an urgent need for political responsibility to counteract some of the dominating effects of modern economics, technology, and power structures, it is an argument balanced by a focus on the possibility of pleasure. She routes her discussion of pleasure through the work of a number of science fiction writers and focuses on it most extensively towards the end of the essay.

Education is another undercurrent throughout the essay. Haraway is keenly attentive to questions of teaching and learning, which she also links to literacy "of several varieties" (not just the capacity to make out words, but the capacity to understand different kinds of symbolism, texts, and ideologies).[1]

Related to this focus on education and literacy is a discussion of writing, or the "etched surfaces of the late twentieth century."[2] Here Haraway seems most closely to follow in the conceptual footsteps of poststructuralist theory, with its keen attention to writing as a

> ❝ Perhaps, ironically, we can learn from our fusions with animals and machines how not to be Man, the embodiment of Western logos. From the point of view of pleasure in these potent and taboo fusions, made inevitable by the social relations of science and technology, there might indeed be a feminist science.
> Donna Haraway, "A Cyborg Manifesto" ❞

technique or a technology. Like Jacques Derrida in *Of Grammatology*, Haraway treats writing as a structure of knowledge that has been dominated by a particular idea of meaning: an essential or original meaning that language is supposed to simply communicate, or "the one code that translates all meaning perfectly."[3] Following Derrida and others—particularly Luce Irigaray—Haraway thinks that it is possible to show that language is characterized by multiplicity and difference, and that feminist writers should struggle to "release" this potential in writing.

Finally, Haraway seems to be interested in the politics of academic writing itself. Her tendency to cite and discuss at length the work of doctoral students in the PhD program at UCSC, and her range of citations in general, seem less focused on establishing a "canon" of authoritative academic voices and more concerned with a sense of open dialogue or the "heteroglossia" she mentions at the end of the essay.

Exploring the Ideas

In some respects, the new possibilities for pleasure that Haraway describes are central to her argument for the political potential of the cyborg myth. Though her focus for much of the essay is on the new possibilities for organization and resistance, the idea of cyborgs as "illegitimate," "infidel," and "blasphemous" all also include a focus on emergent experiences and pleasures, particularly for women. The "taboo fusions" of humans, animals, and machines that are made "inevitable" by the developing technologies also signal a break with repressive boundaries on female pleasure.[4] Haraway affirms the pleasure in connections, skill, and sexual embodiment, all of which can emerge more freely among cyborgs because of the move away from dualisms and the enhancement of capacities.

Against these freer types of pleasure, Haraway contrasts the control exerted by some entertainment technologies, which she sees as part of a general deskilling of the workforce and a tendency to expand certain kinds of illiteracy. Literacy, though, is absolutely crucial to political potential. Like the other kinds of technology that Haraway discusses, writing (and the capacity to read and produce it) is not one-sided. Literacy is a distinguishing marker for the cheap labor hired by multinational companies around the world—here, literacy is not emancipation. However, literacy is also a skill that has been acquired through great struggle by marginalized groups; Haraway writes about poetry and stories by US women of color that are "repeatedly about writing, about access to the power to signify."[5] Crucially, she wants to move away from the dream of unity based on a common language that we are all seeking to find and instead views language as tools that need to be seized.

Overlooked

Haraway's essay has been extremely influential and studied in an exceptionally wide range of contexts. It made the author's name and has become a common text to cite in discussions of contemporary feminism, cultural theory, postmodernism, and the relationship between humans and technology. What is especially striking about the essay itself, and rarely discussed, is her own use of citation. First of all, she cites very widely to contextualize the claims she makes about biotechnological developments, current feminist theory, Marxism, post-structuralism, the changing nature of work, and so on. Second, she gives a prominent place to not-yet-established academics, discussing PhD-qualifying essays and dissertations at length and acknowledging the influence of their ideas. Third, she is scrupulous about citing nonwhite and anti-colonial feminist writers. Fourth, she cites science fiction writers extensively, focusing her attention on women and women of color in particular. All this suggests a deliberate commitment to breaking with at least some of the conventional hierarchies of authority that are embodied in academic citations. Moreover, this practice takes seriously the idea of an educational community: students and faculty at UCSC are among her most important interlocutors. Since she closes the essay with her idea of a multiplicity of "infidel" voices uniting in coalition, it seems clear that Haraway's use of citation is designed to reflect such political commitments in practice.

NOTES

1   Haraway, "A Manifesto for Cyborgs: Science, Technology, and Socialist Feminism in the 1980s," *Socialist Review*, 80 (1985), 89.

2   Haraway, "Manifesto," 95.

3   Haraway, "Manifesto," 95.

4   Haraway, "Manifesto," 92.

5   Haraway, "Manifesto," 93.

MODULE 7
ACHIEVEMENT

KEY POINTS

- "A Cyborg Manifesto" was wildly successful in both its dissemination and influence.

- The make-up of the History of Consciousness Department at the University of California, Santa Cruz was an important context for the nature of the manifesto.

- Donna Haraway's perspective is somewhat limited by its US-American focus, and its style could be considered a mixed blessing.

Assessing the Argument

"A Cyborg Manifesto: Science, Technology, and Socialist-Feminism in the Late Twentieth Century" is a major work of cultural theory that manages to combine breadth and depth of engagement in a variety of different disciplines and discourses with a serious political commitment and an "ironic" tone that makes the work extremely citable. From this point of view, it is a very successful work. Donna Haraway managed to introduce the concept of the cyborg into cultural theory without it being just a gimmick. She also modeled a synthetic or hybrid (or even "cyborg") critical style, yoking together her different discourses and then arguing that just such a multi-voiced style was essential for the politics she was trying to advance.

On Haraway's own terms, to be successful, the work would need to have produced a different mindset towards unity among feminists and socialists (based on coalition and an acceptance of the conditions of "cyborg" existence, or late twentieth-century capitalist society, in other words). The text has certainly been extremely influential in

> **❝** I don't think there's every been a phenomenon like "The Cyborg Manifesto" … Does any major thinker of biopolitics (and I include Michel Foucault in that ascription) bring to the table anything like the range of disciplinary expertise and nimbleness across literatures, discourses, and political communities that we find in Haraway's writing? I don't think so. **❞**
>
> Cary Wolfe, *Manifestly Haraway*

forming attitudes within contemporary cultural theory, though its arguments were divisive among activist groups and have since been criticized for gaps (notably the absence of a sustained treatment of disabled bodies) and shortcomings (for example, being too immersed in US-American culture despite its anti-colonialist claims, or inadvertently marginalizing third-world feminist criticism).

Achievement in Context

Haraway wrote the manifesto in response to a commission from the *Socialist Review*, a long-established quarterly journal of politics and culture which had requested an essay on the current state of socialist feminism in the United States from a number of writers. Haraway had taken up her new tenure-track post at UCSC three years previously, in 1980, and was ultimately granted tenure as a full professor in 1984, the year before the manifesto first appeared.[1] The History of Consciousness Department that Haraway joined is, in some respects, a significant context for the nature of the manifesto. It was a relatively new department, headed by Hayden White* and James Clifford,* and both the program and the faculty were strongly engaged in interdisciplinary research. Haraway taught feminist theory, and there was an emerging engagement in postcolonial theory within the department: Clifford and a number of graduate students established the UCSC Group for the Critical Study of Colonial Discourse in 1984.[2] Fredric Jameson, whose essay "Postmodernism, or the Cultural Logic of Late Capitalism" for *New Left Review* was published in 1984 and was cited approvingly by Haraway, was also a member of the faculty from 1983 to 1985. From this point of view, Haraway's achievement in the essay was partly facilitated by her position in this relatively progressive department, despite the general trajectory of politics in the 1980s being against her.

The editors of the *Socialist Review* were not unanimous in their support of Haraway's essay. In an interview published in 2004, she recalls that the journal's Boston collective considered it politically suspect; they thought that she was celebrating technology uncritically and that her critiques of some feminist theory were anti-feminist.[3] Conversely, the San Francisco collective supported the essay very strongly and pushed through its publication. Early readers of the manifesto recall it as a "phenomenon" spreading widely and being like "the first time you heard a record that really blew you away."[4] The style of the essay proved very popular and was part of its early success.

Limitations

Haraway's manifesto is clearly a text of the 1980s, and more specifically than that, a US-American text of the 1980s. Its citations, while highly varied, are predominantly from US-American writers; its discussion of anti-colonialism refers briefly and generically to "Third World countries" and to nations such as South Korea, but in the context of US-American outsourcing. The active feminist movements with which the text engages are predominantly US-American, and the technological examples Haraway offers are largely from the same context. In short, "A Cyborg Manifesto" is clearly written from a particular perspective, which inevitably places limitations on it.

The style of the manifesto could also be considered a limitation as well as an achievement. By shifting between tones, embracing irony, and developing a complex argument that refuses to either embrace technological developments or treat them as nothing but instruments of domination, the manifesto leaves itself open to readings that either miss these complexities or reject them as too sophisticated (in other words, subtle for the sake of subtlety and therefore losing the effectiveness of direct argument). Even though the style seems to be part of Haraway's aim and politics, the question remains whether it is good politics.

NOTES

1   Donna Haraway and Thyrza Goodeve, *How Like a Leaf: An Interview with Donna Haraway* (New York: Routledge, 2000), 177.

2   Christopher Leigh Connery, "Worlded Pedagogy in Santa Cruz," in *The Worlding Project: Doing Cultural Studies in the Era of Globalization*, ed. Rob Wilson and Christopher Leigh Connery (Santa Cruz: New Pacific Books, 2007), 5.

3   Donna Haraway, Nina Lykke, Randi Markussen, and Finn Olesen, "Cyborgs, coyotes, and dogs: a kinship of feminist figurations" and "There are always more things going on than you thought! Methodologies as thinking technologies," in *The Haraway Reader* (New York: Routledge, 2004), 324.

4   Carey Wolfe, "Introduction," in Donna J. Haraway, *Manifestly Haraway* (Minneapolis: University of Minnesota Press, 2016), vii.

PLACE IN THE AUTHOR'S WORK

KEY POINTS

- The phenomenal success of "A Cyborg Manifesto" gave Donna Haraway an international reputation as a leading feminist and cultural theorist.

- Its interdisciplinary focus means that it synthesizes many of Haraway's interests and commitments in one relatively short piece.

- The very success of the manifesto may have skewed the reception of Haraway's other work, which is worth reading in its own right.

Positioning

"A Cyborg Manifesto: Science, Technology, and Socialist-Feminism in the Late Twentieth Century" was originally published shortly after Donna Haraway received tenure at the University of California, Santa Cruz, and by the time she wrote it, she already had an emerging academic reputation in feminist theory and interdisciplinary cultural studies. Her work was being published in international journals and appearing in translation by the early 1980s. Her first book, *Crystals, Fabrics, and Fields: Metaphors of Organicism in Twentieth-Century Developmental Biology*, had been published in 1976 and received tentative but relatively favorable reviews in such major scientific journals as *Science* and *The British Journal for the History of Science*.[1] In short, Haraway was a relatively established academic by the time she wrote the manifesto.

However, the reception of "A Cyborg Manifesto" was transformative for Haraway's international reputation and is the text for which she is most famous—indeed, for many readers, she will be synonymous with this text and less known for any of her other work. Much of Haraway's

> **❝** The refusal of an atomistic approach is key to reading Haraway's work in general ... Haraway agrees: 'When people miss the relations, the whole, and focus only on separate bits, they come up with all sorts of misreadings of my work' ... This is an important caution for those who read the 'Cyborg Manifesto' stripped of its socialist feminism. **❞**
>
> Margaret Grebowicz and Helen Merrick, *Beyond the Cyborg: Adventures with Donna Haraway*

subsequent research developed her interest in the boundaries and relationships between humans, animals, and machines, with animal–human relations becoming more central in her later work.

Integration

"A Cyborg Manifesto" is a highly integrated text already, in the sense that it synthesizes many aspects of Haraway's interdisciplinary academic background to advance its argument. It is important to see the work as part of a wider academic context that was increasingly open to interdisciplinary research, with the History of Consciousness Department at UCSC particularly receptive to such approaches. More broadly, her work is linked to the development of interdisciplinary cultural studies as an established academic field in the United States.

Because of its interdisciplinary focus and its political commitments to feminism, postcolonialism, and socialism, the manifesto brought together many of Haraway's diverse interests in one place. Her later work maintains similar interests, and so the essay can be productively read in the context of books like *Primate Visions: Gender, Race, and Nature in the World of Modern Science* (1989), *When Species Meet* (2008), and most recently *Staying with the Trouble: Making Kin in the Cthulucene* (2016), all of which adapt and develop some of the ideas that appear in the manifesto. Environmental threats, the fragility of ecosystems, interspecies connection, and the idea of kinship all become increasingly important in these texts.

Significance

"A Cyborg Manifesto" is by far Haraway's most significant work in terms of citation, recognition, and general influence. The ideas have been widely and repeatedly discussed, and the text is a touchstone for learning about feminist theory, science studies, interdisciplinary cultural studies, postmodernism, and intersectional political theory. In a way, the manifesto's success somewhat overshadows Haraway's subsequent work and achievements, even though it also helped to widen her readership and cement her authority as a leading name in feminist cultural studies. Partly because of the impact of the cyborg essay, Haraway's later work includes a number of texts in which she responds to its reception, taking a critical position on ideas like posthumanism* and cyberfeminism,* both of which drew on her ideas in the manifesto.

Although the manifesto is a foundational work for courses in "cyborg studies" or, more recently, "cyborg anthropology," these are relatively niche subfields of cultural studies and anthropology. The real significance of the text has been to influence the language and philosophical basis of these larger disciplines. The essay has been criticized as well as celebrated, but although the truth and value of some of Haraway's ideas remain open to question, her basic premises and the significance of the manifesto have not been discredited and are still regarded as worthwhile avenues of inquiry.

NOTES

1 Mikuláš Teich, "Review," *The British Journal for the History of Science*, 11.1 (1978), 92–4; J.T. Bonner, "Review," Science, 193.4252 (1976), 477–8.

SECTION 3
IMPACT

THE FIRST RESPONSES

KEY POINTS

* "A Cyborg Manifesto" was controversial from the beginning, but also read and critiqued with care by other feminist theorists in the early phase of its reception.

* Donna Haraway has responded to the reception of the manifesto on a number of occasions since its publication, often in published interviews.

* Overenthusiastic misinterpretations of Haraway's ideas in the manifesto have been just as much a source of conflict as criticisms of it, if not more so.

Criticism

"A Cyborg Manifesto: Science, Technology, and Socialist-Feminism in the Late Twentieth Century" was controversial even before it reached publication. The *Socialist Review*, which ultimately published the essay, had two separate editorial groups: a Boston collective and a San Francisco collective. The Boston editors were critical of what they perceived as anti-feminism and an uncritical celebration of technology in Haraway's essay.

After publication, the essay gained a phenomenally wide readership in a relatively short space of time. Responses to it varied in depth and care, but some early criticisms of the manifesto were offered by feminist scholars who were broadly sympathetic to Haraway's aims. Notably, responses to the manifesto by Christina Crosby, Mary Ann Doane,* and Joan W. Scott* were published in 1989 in a collection entitled *Coming to Terms: Feminism, Theory, Politics*. These essays had originally been presented at a 1986 colloquium on Haraway's manifesto that she herself had attended and so constitute a very early

> ❝ For Burke, liberal democracy is an achievement of
> Western civilization, refined and improved gradually
> over many generations ... For Paine, liberal democracy
> is the application of principles discovered in the
> Enlightenment. It's a break, a sharp break, from
> everything that preceded the Enlightenment, and the
> purpose of politics is to further apply those principles ...
> And there you have the foundation of conservatism on
> the one hand and progressivism on the other.❞[1]
>
> Yuval Levin*, quoted in Nat Brown, "Edmund Burke v. Thomas Paine"

response to the text from different perspectives in feminist theory.

Crosby's critique is that Haraway's focus on inclusiveness and coalition risks coming at the expense of a politics of exclusion: the capacity to "make the right connections and block the wrong ones," such as being able to say that "the porn industry in general [is] (how can I put it?) the enemy."[1] Crosby writes that Haraway had taken these considerations into account, but she wanted to be cautious about how the figure of the cyborg—with its broken boundaries and capacity to connect to everything—should be interpreted. Doane argues, from a perspective rooted in psychoanalytic theory, that Haraway's rejection of ideas of origin means that her essay risks losing sight of the importance of loss in feminist theory. She suggests that the manifesto lacks a real theory of subjectivity; it is too caught up in the utopian "myth" that Haraway describes.[2] Scott focuses on "traces of an older mode of analysis not entirely displaced" in the essay: an implicit economic or technological determinism* and (most damningly) a romanticization of women of color, both of which she associates with traditional socialism.[3]

Responses

The success of the manifesto meant that Haraway had many opportunities to respond to initial criticisms. In addition to attending colloquia specifically devoted to the essay, she has appeared in a number of published interviews over the past 30 years. One from 1990 with Constance Penley* and Andrew Ross* in Social Text is worth noting in this context, since the interviewers paraphrase the kind of critique advanced by Doane and Scott—in particular, the lack of a psychoanalytic perspective, meaning that there is no real sense of subjectivity, and the risk of romanticizing women of color to suit Haraway's own rhetorical purposes. To the first question, Haraway jokes that she is less of a "fundamentalist" about psychoanalysis than in 1985, but insists that the existing ideas that have been used to describe the unconscious (notably the Oedipus myth*) are "much too conservative, much too heterosexist, much too familiar, much too exclusive."[4] The interviewers press her further on this, suggesting that getting rid of certain psychoanalytic ideas would weaken our understanding of how racism works, citing authors like Frantz Fanon* and Homi Bhabha.* Haraway agrees in general but suggests that the concepts and categories of psychoanalysis are too rigid and need redefining—perhaps through the cyborg fictions of a science-fiction writer like Octavia Butler. To the second question, Haraway concedes that her essay "partly ends up further imperializing" some of the working-class women of color she mentions. She notes that she would be "much more careful about describing who counts as a 'we,' in the statement, 'we are all cyborgs'." Drawing on the work of Aiwha Ong,* she gives a brief account of Malaysian factory workers whose complex and contradictory circumstances would make the name "cyborg" inappropriate.[5]

Conflict and Consensus

The interview with Penley and Ross is a useful reference point for Haraway's response to early criticisms of the manifesto, since it shows her both open to revising parts of it and dogged about some of her premises. Early respondents to the essay like Christina Crosby, Doane, Scott, and Sandra Harding* seem to be testing out the implications of Haraway's arguments in relation to the existing paradigms of feminist and socialist cultural theory. In Zoë Sofoulis's* words, "A Cyborg Manifesto" was a kind of earthquake that "jolted many out of their categorical certainties as it shifted the terrain of debate about culture and identity in the late twentieth century."[6]

On the whole, it was not so much criticism of the manifesto that was a problem for Haraway but some of the less careful and more celebratory interpretations of what she had written. From a certain point of view, these interpretations had a greater influence on debates about the manifesto through the 1990s and into the twenty-first century. The conflict generated by the text was just as much about how it had been misread in a "positive" light as it had been in a "critical" one. In a 1996 interview with Gary Olson,* for example, reflecting on the reception of the manifesto, she talks of being irked that a number of people read her as "some blissed-out, cyborg propagandist."[7]

NOTES

1 Christina Crosby, "Commentary: Allies and Enemies," in Coming to Terms: Feminism, Theory, Politics, ed. Elizabeth Weed (London: Routledge, 1989), 208.

2 Mary Ann Doane, "Commentary: Post-Utopian Difference," in Coming to Terms, 210.

3 Joan W. Scott, "Commentary: Cyborgian Socialists," in Coming to Terms, 216.

4 Constance Penley, Andrew Ross, and Donna Haraway, "Cyborgs at Large: Interview with Donna Haraway," Social Text, 25–6 (1990), 8–23, 15.

5 Penley et al., "Cyborgs at Large," 17.

6   Zoë Sofoulis, "Cyberquake: Haraway's Manifesto," in Prefiguring
     Cyberculture: An Intellectual History, ed. Darren Tofts, Annemarie Jonson,
     and Alessio Cavallaro (Cambridge: MIT Press, 2002), 84–103, 84.

7   Gary A. Olson, "Writing, Literacy and Technology: Toward a Cyborg Writing,"
     JAC, 16.1 (1996), 1–26, 25.

MODULE 10
THE EVOLVING DEBATE

KEY POINTS

- Part of Donna Haraway's point in "A Cyborg Manifesto" was that "using" the figure of the cyborg involved necessary tensions and difficulties. This has not always been understood in the essay's reception.

- The manifesto has influenced intersectional politics, queer theory* and transgender studies,* posthumanism, cyberfeminism, and feminist theory in general.

- In current scholarship, some of the most striking developments and critiques of Haraway's ideas have been made by former students in the History of Consciousness Department at UCSC where she taught.

Uses and Problems

"A Cyborg Manifesto: Science, Technology, and Socialist-Feminism in the Late Twentieth Century" attained a life of its own and has been used by readers from a very wide variety of different fields. This makes it very difficult to chart a linear history of how Donna Haraway's ideas have been applied. In a sense, the promiscuous use of the work is perhaps one of the most significant characteristics of the evolving debate around it. Above all, the cyborg has proven to be a useful "myth": Haraway established the cyborg as a credible—if contested—way of thinking about the relationship between humans and technology. The idea of humans as cyborgs has been picked up by many subsequent writers, some of them doing justice to the tensions in Haraway's essay, others less careful in their use of her language and concepts.

In the manifesto, Haraway treated the cyborg as a potentially useful

> 66 [T]he cyborg is from the start a polluted category ...
> It's an offspring of World War II nuclear culture, and
> there's no possibility of working out of that position to
> imagine yourself in the Garden of Eden or returning to
> pre-Oedipal bliss ... You have to take your implication
> in a fraught world as the starting point. 99
>
> Donna Haraway, Interview with Gary Olson

figure for rebellion and resistance, but one that was also already implicated in control, domination, and colonization. The very point of the essay was that "using" the cyborg was fraught with risk, since it meant accepting the conditions of domination (work and leisure being colonized and controlled by technological development) as a starting point for action. This is perhaps one of the reasons why Haraway observes, in a later interview, "I think that as an oppositional figure the cyborg has a rather short half-life (laughter)."[1] Implicitly, the very popularity of the manifesto and the ways the cyborg-figure has been used have contributed to a loss of what radical potential it once had.

Schools of Thought

"A Cyborg Manifesto" provided a language and a conceptual framework for theories of intersectionality, as in the work of Nina Lykke.[*2] Its utopian myth of cyborg pleasure and connections was adopted by queer and transgender studies as a useful way of thinking about technology, and because Haraway understood the cyborg as a figure that fundamentally destabilizes heterosexual hierarchies (a notable example is Jack Halberstam's* work from the early 1990s).[3]

The idea of hybridity and a porous boundary between human and nonhuman (animal or machine) have been used to help explain the concept of posthumanism, notably in Katherine Hayles's* work, even though Haraway has herself been critical of the term.[4]   Similarly, theorists of cyberfeminism drew on the manifesto's critique of technophobia and systematically misinterpreted it as a justification of the idea that "it's possible to construct your identity, your sexuality, even your gender, just as you please."

More broadly, Haraway's manifesto was influential in various fields of feminist inquiry, especially those having to do with labor and work, science and technology, and identity politics in general. The manifesto provided a language and a set of concepts that helped to get feminist debates of the 1980s out of an impasse in their conflicts over essential femininity and multiple feminisms.[5]

In Current Scholarship
Many of the graduate students who studied in the History of Consciousness Department at UCSC in the 1980s with Haraway and the other faculty members became established scholars in their own right, and in some cases their research responds more or less directly to the manifesto. In current scholarship, this work often intersects with further technological developments since the 1980s. Katie King's Networked Reenactments (2011) aims to build on Haraway's notion of "feminist technoscience"; T. V. Reed's* Digitized Lives: Culture, Power, and Social Change in the Internet Era (2014) includes a chapter dedicated to cyborg theory and online privacy; Caren Kaplan's* co-edited volume Life in the Age of Drone Warfare (2017) cites the manifesto in its effort to explore "the gendered dynamics of unmanned systems."

Haraway cites Chela Sandoval's concept of oppositional consciousness extensively in her essay. In her important monograph, Methodology of the Oppressed (2000), Sandoval returns to the manifesto and offers a significant critique: by using US-American third-world feminist criticism to illustrate the idea of "cyborg feminism," the manifesto tends to absorb, domesticate, and ultimately marginalize or even colonize the specific contributions of these other writers. Sandoval indicates that this is written into the logic of the essay despite Haraway's best intentions and alliances with feminists of color. It was exacerbated by the reception of the cyborg, which became such a powerful concept across so many fields that it flattened the specificities of differential feminism. Interestingly, Sandoval suggests that a later essay of Haraway's ("Ecce Homo," 1992) shows a development in her thinking that is more productive for oppositional politics than the cyborg essay; she appreciates Haraway's work while trying to expose the limitations of her most popular, not to say hegemonic, essay.[6]

NOTES

1   Donna Haraway, Nina Lykke, Randi Markussen, and Finn Olesen, "Cyborgs, coyotes, and dogs: a kinship of feminist figurations" and "There are always more things going on than you thought! Methodologies as thinking technologies," in *The Haraway Reader* (New York: Routledge, 2004), 326.

2   Nina Lykke, *Feminist Studies: A Guide to Intersectional Theory, Methodology and Writing* (New York: Routledge, 2011).

3   Judith Halberstam, "Automating Gender: Postmodern Feminism in the Age of the Intelligent Machine," *Feminist Studies*, 17.3 (1991), 439–60; *Skin Shows: Gothic Horror and the Technology of Monsters* (Durham: Duke UP, 1995).

4   N. Katherine Hayles, How We Became Posthuman: Virtual Bodies in Cybernetics, Literature, and Informatics (Chicago: U. of Chicago Press); Gane and Haraway, "Interview," 140.

5   Zoë Sofoulis, "Cyberquake: Haraway's Manifesto," in *Prefiguring Cyberculture: An Intellectual History*, ed. Darren Tofts, Annemarie Jonson, and Alessio Cavallaro (Cambridge: MIT Press, 2002), passim.

6   Chela Sandoval, *Methodology of the Oppressed* (Minneapolis: U. of Minnesota Press, 2000), 171.

IMPACT AND INFLUENCE TODAY

KEY POINTS

- "A Cyborg Manifesto" is a seminal work and a cult work—both of these things may have contributed to a loss of the radical potential that the figure of the cyborg once had.

- On the other hand, the manifesto continues to provide a powerful and engaging theoretical framework. It is important to remember how provoking and illuminating it can be.

- The most interesting, sharpest critiques of Donna Haraway have to do with how she treats race and disability in the manifesto, despite her best intentions.

Position

"A Cyborg Manifesto: Science, Technology, and Socialist-Feminism in the Late Twentieth Century" is widely recognized as both a seminal essay and a cult text—in other words, a work that had an immense impact on a number of different fields, and also one that gained widespread popularity. The cult status of the essay is, for Chela Sandoval and for Donna Haraway herself, one reason why the cyborg figure has lost its political potential: In women's studies and academic feminism, it has become simply another identity category, an explanatory concept that domesticates (reduces and makes familiar, and ultimately absorbs) the specific differences, experiences, theories, and activist methods of third-world feminism.

On the other hand, the manifesto still provides a basis for research into the new biotechnologies and communication technologies that pervade early twenty-first century human experience. Equally, despite the critiques, its status as a cult text should not necessarily be seen

> ❝ Much of Haraway's work thus has been to identify the technical skills required for producing a dissident global movement and human being that are capable of generating egalitarian and just social relations. The skills she identifies are equivalent to the technologies I have identified in this book as the methodology of the oppressed ❞
>
> Harvey Kaye, quoted in Brendan O'Neill, "Who Was Thomas Paine?"

straightforwardly as a bad thing: Sophie Lewis's* 2017 essay for *Viewpoint Magazine* recalls the author's first encounter with the manifesto as a teenager, its "baroque, yet pellucid" style, a "witchy" writing that "felt like coming home."[1] For Lewis, Haraway's manifesto produced a desire for just the kind of activist connection—and literacy— that it describes.

Interaction

T Lewis's essay for Viewpoint is in fact a sharp critique of Haraway's most recent book, *Staying with the Trouble: Making Kin in the Chthulucene* (2016). Lewis recounts defending Haraway's work against all the usual critiques ("self-indulgence, stylistic obscurantism, 'postmodern' triviality, etymological shamanism"), continuing to find it provoking and illuminating. But *Staying with the Trouble* marks a departure: Lewis argues that it is consumed by populationism, a desire to radically decrease the world's population in response to ecological disaster. Lewis quotes the "Companion Species Manifesto" (2003), where Haraway writes that "I have come to see cyborgs as junior siblings in the much bigger, queer family of companion species."[2] But Lewis's final point is that the cyborg actually seems a much more useful concept, still, than Haraway's more recent arguments. In other words, Lewis argues for the ongoing inspiration of the manifesto, even against its author's current thinking.

Otherwise, many academic writers working in a variety of fields continue to interact with "A Cyborg Manifesto," from Rosi Braidotti's* exploration of the "critical posthumanities" to Eben Kirksey's* "emergent ecologies."[3] It continues to provide a conceptual framework, even where Haraway's ideas in the essay are not discussed at length.

The Continuing Debate

Where contemporary scholars do engage closely with the manifesto, it is most commonly to explore some of the gaps and tensions in it.

Chief among these is the criticism advanced by Joan W. Scott and Chela Sandroval: that Haraway assimilates women of color into the category of "cyborg" in a way that inadvertently perpetuates the very marginalization that she is arguing against. A recent extension of this argument is Malini Johar Schueller's* discussion of the cyborg in *Locating Race: Global Sites of Post-Colonial Citizenship* (2009). Schueller writes that Haraway's attempt to develop an inclusive feminist activism "is to be lauded," but that it disregards and flattens the historical specificity of the "women of color" Haraway repeatedly names. This means that it "avails itself of the universalizing and unmarked privileges of whiteness" and helps to "defuse … or deny the responsibility of working with whiteness"—in other words, conceptualizing women or feminists as cyborgs tends to get rid of exactly the effort and the discomfort of coalition that Bernice Reagon described in the essay on coalition politics that inspires Haraway's argument.

In her book *Feminist, Queer, Crip* (2013), Alison Kafer* argues that this criticism of the manifesto on the grounds of race is correct, and yet it reveals a significant gap: While feminists have "the tools and the training" to recognize a misuse of race and class, they do not have the same familiarity with representations of disability to notice that Haraway—in Kafer's view—does something equally suspect when she writes that "perhaps paraplegics and other severely handicapped people can (and sometimes do) have the most intense experiences of complex hybridization."*⁴ The fact that this is a brief aside is part of the problem, but the really revealing thing, for Kafer, is that in all the many years of responses to Haraway's manifesto, the treatment of disability has barely registered. Not just Haraway herself but her readers as well are implicated.

Neither Schueller nor Kafer condemns the manifesto out of hand, but these are some of the sharpest critiques that have been made against it, particularly given its influential status in theories of intersectionality. Their argument suggests that the manifesto is not intersectional enough in its perspective.

NOTES

1   Sophie Lewis, "Cthulhu plays no role for me," *Viewpoint Magazine*, 8 May 2017.

2   Donna Haraway, *The Companion Species Manifesto: Dogs, People, and Significant Otherness* (Chicago: Prickly Paradigm Press, 2003), 11.

3   Rosi Braidotti, "A Theoretical Framework for the Critical Posthumanities," *Theory, Culture & Society*, 0(0) (2018), 1–31; Eben Kirksey, *Emergent Ecologies* (Durham: Duke UP, 2015).

4   Donna Haraway, "A Cyborg Manifesto," 97; cited in Alison Kafer, *Feminist, Queer, Crip* (Bloomington: Indiana UP, 2013), 105.

WHERE NEXT?

KEY POINTS

- "A Cyborg Manifesto" will continue to be recognized as a classic essay in its own right as well as for its influence on a variety of fields.

- Future work may use Donna Haraway's conceptual framework to explore the impact of new technological developments that blend organisms and machines.

- But it could also focus on careful rereading of the manifesto to really understand both the potential and the problems of the cyborg figure.

Potential

It seems highly likely that "A Cyborg Manifesto: Science, Technology, and Socialist-Feminism in the Late Twentieth Century" will continue to be read and cited as an influential essay and reference point in a number of different fields. It has been cited so widely that there is a kind of critical mass around it which makes it almost impossible to avoid. More importantly, it is very difficult to understand the development of feminist theory, cultural studies, research into the history and philosophy of science, intersectional politics, or other fields like posthumanism, queer theory, and even ecocriticism,* without encountering the influence of Donna Haraway's manifesto. It is possible to read and assimilate the ideas of the essay without engaging closely with the secondary literature or such keen critiques as those of Malini Johar Schueller and Alison Kafer, though in order to gain a deeper and more critical understanding of contemporary debates in feminism, they are important. Since the economic, technological, and social dynamics that Haraway describes in the manifesto have not only

> ❝ [A]re drones* today's cyborgs? For Haraway the cyborg was 'the illegitimate offspring of militarism and patriarchal capitalism' ... [The drone] is of a new generation, born in the age of the algorithm. The drone furthers the cyborg's dream of absolute knowledge, as it emblemizes fantasies of data-driven power in a time of increasing environmental vulnerability and capitalist collapse. ❞
>
> Anna Feigenbaum,* "From cyborg feminism to drone feminism: Remembering women's anti-nuclear activisms"

persisted but intensified and accelerated—from a certain perspective, at least—her analysis of the emerging conditions of lived experience in the 1980s is still pertinent. Furthermore, the kinds of political consciousness raised by Black Lives Matter* and other mass social media movements have brought to the center of attention similar questions about identity, affiliation, and alliance to the ones that Haraway tries to negotiate in the manifesto

Future Directions
The work of UCSC graduates like Katie King, T.V. Reed, and Caren Kaplan suggests one possible future direction of work on Haraway's manifesto. Their most recent books all explore more recent technological developments and their relationship to economics and social experience: the expansion of networks and the role of the internet in everyday life as well as the coming of drones in both military and "civilian" contexts. In this context, a significant essay by an emerging scholar is Anna Feigenbaum's "From cyborg feminism to drone feminism: Remembering women's anti-nuclear activisms" (2015). Haraway briefly explores the Greenham Common* anti-nuclear protestors in her manifesto, part of the essay's wider critique of militarism and the cyborg's involvement in war. Feigenbaum goes

back to 1980s anti-militarist feminism in order to advance an argument for emergent feminist activist movements to understand and contest the expansion of drone surveillance and remote killing.[1]

Sophie Lewis's Viewpoint essay is also suggestive in its call for a return to "A Cyborg Manifesto"—or rather, the other way around: "What if the cyborgs made a comeback? They knew who their enemies were."[2] Her essay is striking because of the way it calls for a re-reading of Haraway's manifesto, recalling the surprise and the potential for new connections that it could produce, even if it now seems so familiar in academic discourse as to only need a passing mention. If this call to revisit the political potential of the cyborg figure is to be taken seriously, the counterpart would have to be a serious engagement with the sharp critiques made by Schueller, Kafer, and others, reading the manifesto in the light of current debates around intersectionality.

Summary

"A Cyborg Manifesto" is a stylish, serious, committed, and intellectually challenging piece of writing that has had a remarkable reception history. It continues to be influential in a wide variety of academic fields, from certain corners of anthropology, sociology, and geography to the humanities disciplines of literary and cultural studies, feminist theory, and the history of science and technology. More than that, it has had an impact on popular culture and been read as much by artists and activists as by students and academics. The work has become familiar by recitation, but this may cause some readers to overlook the knots and tensions in it, which means that a careful (re)reading is essential to consider both its usefulness and its problems.

NOTES

1   Anna Feigenbaum, "From cyborg feminism to drone feminism: Remembering women's anti-nuclear activisms," *Feminist Theory*, 16.3 (2015), 265–88.

2   Sophie Lewis, "Cthulhu plays no role for me," *Viewpoint Magazine*, 8 May 2017.

GLOSSARY

GLOSSARY OF TERMS

Biotechnology: the application and manipulation of biological science and technology to produce products and applications that enhance living organisms.

Black Lives Matter: an activist movement that began in the US African-American community in 2013 and campaigns against violence and structural racism against black people.

Catholic Church: also called the Roman Catholic Church, this is the largest branch of Christianity and is headed by the Pope in Rome. The Catholic Church was formed in the fourth century c.e. and since then, several groups have broken with Catholicism to form their own denominations, such as Christian Orthodoxy (formed in the eleventh century) and Protestantism (formed in the sixteenth century).

Catholic Left: not a defined movement, but a recognized part of Catholic* culture that combines left-wing or broadly socialist politics with Christian ethics and theology.

Cultural studies: a field of academic study that began at the University of Birmingham in the 1960s and was then widely taken up and adapted in US academia during the 1970s and 1980s. Broadly, cultural studies describes a consciously open and interdisciplinary approach to analyzing cultural practices of all kind.

Cyberfeminism: a term coined in the early 1990s to describe an approach to feminist* theory and practice that was especially interested in cybernetics, technology, and new information technologies such as the internet.

Deindustrialization: the reduction of industrial activity in a nation or region, sometimes associated with outsourcing* and offshoring* of production and manufacturing.

Determinism: the philosophical view that human activity is not free but determined by external forces acting upon the person.

Digital economy: a term used to describe an economy based on digital technologies, especially computing and the internet.

Drones: remote controlled, pilotless aircraft, sometimes called an unmanned aerial vehicle (UAV).

Dualism: system of thought that is based on pairs of opposing, independent ideas.

Ecocriticism: a field of interdisciplinary study focused on representations of the natural world, particularly in the context of modern concerns about ecological destruction.

Epistemology: the branch of philosophy concerned with exploring the nature and conditions of knowledge and understanding.

Feminism: a series of ideologies and movements concerned with equal social, political, cultural, and economic rights for women, including equal rights in the home, workplace, education, and government.

Feminist sex wars: sometimes known as the "porn wars," a debate among feminists* in the late 1970s and 1980s broadly focused on attitudes towards sexuality.

Fulbright scholarship: a cultural exchange program established in 1946 which provides funding for U citizens to study, research, and teach in other countries, and for citizens of other countries to do so in the US.

Gender theory: an interdisciplinary method for understanding gender relations, gender identity, and sexual orientation, including how gender and sexual orientation are perceived and/or represented in culture.

Greenham Common: a former Royal Air Force base in Berkshire England, where in 1981 the Greenham Common Women's Peace Camp was established to protest against nuclear weapons being placed at the base. In 1982 it was decided that the protests should involve only women. The camp was active for 19 years and was disbanded in 2000.

Heteroglossia: from the Greek for "other" (hetero-) and "tongue" (glossa), a word used in literary theory to describe the synthesis of multiple voices in a text.

Hybridization: the formation of hybrids—these being anything made up of multiple different or incongruous elements.

Interdisciplinary: a word used to describe academic research that involves theories or methods from more than one established discipline.

Intersectionality (intersectional): a term used to describe a framework for thinking about how different kinds of people are marginalized or oppressed within a society and to advocate a perspective that is careful about those differences. It is deliberately opposed to narrower, identity-focused political movements, such as earlier forms of feminism that tended to exclude consideration of, for example, race, class, sexuality or disability.

Left: an umbrella term used to refer to left-wing politics and political movements such as republicanism, socialism and social democracy. The Left usually promotes social equality and egalitarianism and commonly opposes social hierarchy.

Marxism: refers to cultural, philosophical, socio-economic, political, and aesthetic readings based on the work of the nineteenth-century political economist Karl Marx. Marxist theorists and writers are concerned with the growth of social inequality under capitalism, and the influence this has on culture and society.

Oedipus myth: in Greek mythology, king of Thebes who discovered that he had unknowingly married his mother. In the context of psychoanalysis, it is used by Sigmund Freud to describe the conflicted relationship that a child has to its parents.

Offshoring: a word coined in the 1980s to describe the process of moving a business or parts of a business to another country, usually to benefit from lower costs.

Ontology: the branch of philosophy concerned with exploring the nature and conditions of being or existence.

Oppositional consciousness: a collective mental state of struggle, negotiation and contest by which a subordinate group can challenge the dominant group or discourse in society.

Outsourcing: a word coined in the late 1970s to describe the business practice of employing people outside of a business to do work for that business – otherwise known as contracting out.

Patriarchal: in general, an adjective describing a structure of society in which men dominate positions of authority, and in which cultural assumptions often privilege men or masculinity over women.

Phallogocentrism: a word coined by Jacques Derrida* and commonly used in post-structuralist* feminist* theory, describing a structure of thought and language that tends to reinforce male dominance.

Posthumanism: philosophical term interpreted in various ways but referring in general to a critical perspective towards the conventional principles of humanism.

Postmodernism (postmodern): in general, a set of social and cultural conditions that come after what is considered modern or modernist. Sometimes used to describe a style in art or literature, and sometimes to describe a more pervasive set of dominant social and cultural conditions. In both cases, postmodernism is characterized by plurality and a breaking down of borders.

Post-structuralism (post-structuralist): a broad set of philosophical perspectives associated especially with twentieth-century continental (European) philosophy and characterized by a critical approach towards dualisms and binary oppositions, an intense focus on language, a keen attention to the idea of difference, and a skepticism towards concepts such as essence, spirit, or origin.

Primatology: the scientific study of primates including monkeys, apes, lemurs, and lorisids.

Queer theory: a branch of cultural and critical theory that developed in the early 1990s, initially associated with gay rights activism and developing a philosophical perspective that focuses on ambiguity and undecidability.

Radical feminism: A branch of feminism dedicated to overthrowing existing political and social structures because of the way in which they structurally oppress women.

Reagan Doctrine: a strategy under the Ronald Reagan* presidential administration (1981–89) to expand US global influence and undermine the influence of the Soviet Union. Principally, it involved offering support to anti-communist movements and opposing governments sympathetic towards communism. It included a major focus on increasing the military strength of the US.

Second-wave feminism: emerging out of the women's rights and women's liberation movements of the 1960s, second-wave feminism was characterized by systematic questioning and critique of established gender roles with the aim of campaigning for greater equality.

Silicon Valley: the name given to the Santa Clara Valley in the San Francisco Bay Area, Northern California, because of the prevalence of technology and computing companies established there (silicon being the material used in commercial semiconductors for electronic devices).

Simulacrum: in general, a copy or an image of something, especially one that lacks the substance or qualities of the original. In postmodernist* theory, it is used to describe a copy that has no original.

Socialist: one who believes in the collective ownership of the means of production and the collective management of the economy.

Socialist-Feminism: An offshoot of feminism which draws on socialist* principles, arguing that capitalist societies are inherently unequal to women, and so gender equality can only be achieved under more equal social conditions.

Sputnik: the name of the first satellite sent by humans into space by the Soviet Union's space program in 1957.

Strategic Defense Initiative: nicknamed the Star Wars program, a proposed missile defense system for the US that would have used high-technology weapons, including lasers, fired from satellites to knock out any ballistic missile fired at the United States.

Taylorism: a systematic approach to organizing labor in order to maximize efficiency and productivity, associated with deskilling—the mechanization or computerization of a task to the degree that the human skill required to complete the task is minimal or becomes obsolete—because it encouraged a division of work in which each individual performs simple, repetitive tasks.

Technoscience: in this context, a term that refers specifically to the technological and social context in which science is practiced.

Teleology: a philosophical principle or branch of study that focuses on ends, goals, or final causes.

Transgender studies: a field of interdisciplinary research that focuses on the culture, lived experience, and representation of transgender people and communities.

Vietnam Syndrome: phrase used by Ronald Reagan* to describe a widespread antagonism in the United States towards overseas military action following the experience of the Vietnam War. Reagan talked of it as something to be overcome.

PEOPLE MENTIONED IN THE TEXT

Jean Baudrillard (1929-2007) was a French theorist of postmodern society and culture. He most famously argued that simulation and play are critical components of the postmodern* social order. Key works include Simulation and Simulacra (1994) and America (1988).

Homi K. Bhabha (b. 1949) is a professor English and American literature and language at Harvard University. His work has focused on postcolonial theory and questions of hybridity, which he began developing in his first book, The Location of Culture (1994).

Rosi Braidotti (b. 1954) is a feminist philosopher and Distinguished University Professor at Utrecht University. Her work has been primarily concerned with the tension between identity and difference, developed in texts such as Nomadic Subjects (1994) and Metamorphoses (2002).

Octavia Butler (1947-2006) was an award-winning African-American science fiction writer whose work includes the Patternist series (1976-1984) and her breakthrough novel, Kindred (1979).

James Clifford (b. 1945) is an interdisciplinary historian based at the University of California, Santa Cruz where he was the founding director of the Center for Cultural Studies and is Distinguished Professor in the Humanities and Emeritus Professor in the History of Consciousness Department.

Christina Crosby (b. 1953) is a professor of English, feminist, gender and sexuality studies at Wesleyan University whose most recent work has focused on disability studies.

Samuel R. Delaney (b. 1942) is an award-winning African American science fiction novelist and short story writer whose works include *Babel-17* (1966) and the *Return to Nevèrÿon* series (1979-1987). He held various university appointments, most recently as professor of English and creative writing at Temple University.

Jacques Derrida (1930-2004) was a French Algerian theorist who developed the critical approach of deconstruction for literary analysis. His key works include *Speech and Phenomena* (1967), *Of Grammatology* (1976), and *Writing and Difference* (1978).

Mary Ann Doane (b. 1952) is the Class of 1937 Professor of Film and Media at the University of California, Berkeley whose work has focused on women and film in publications such as *The Desire to Desire* (1987) and *Femmes Fatales* (1991).

Frantz Fanon (1925-1961) was born in Martinique and trained as a medic in France before working first in Tunisia and then in Algeria. His thinking through of race with psychoanalysis as developed in *Black Skin, White Masks* (1952) is a key to anti-colonial thought.

Anna Feigenbaum is the Principal Academic in Digital Storytelling at Bournemouth University. Her interdisciplinary work looks at the intersection of technology and political activism. She is co-author of the book Protest Camps (2013).

Michel Foucault (1926-1984) was a French theorist and philosopher concerned with the history of categories. His works include *The Archaeology of Knowledge* (1969) and *The History of Sexuality* (1976-1984). He was professor of philosophy at the *Experimental University of Paris VIII* (Vincennes).

Susan Griffin (b. 1943) is a US-American feminist writer whose first book *Woman and Nature* (1978) is often taken as a foundational moment of ecofeminism.

Jack Halberstam (b. 1961) is a professor of English and Comparative Literature at Columbia University whose work on gender variance as developed in such books as *Female Masculinity* (1998) and *The Queer Art of Failure* (2011) has been crucial to the development of queer studies. Her earlier work was published under the name Judith Halberstam.

Sandra Harding (b. 1935) is Distinguished Professor Emerita of Education and Gender Studies at the University of California, Los Angeles. Her work in the philosophy of science and feminist epistemology contributed to standpoint methodology in studies such as *Whose Science? Whose Knowledge?* (1991).

Nancy Hartsock (1943-2015) was a US-American feminist philosopher who was a professor of political science at the University of Washington. Her essay "The Feminist Standpoint" (1983) was crucial to early feminist epistemology.

N. Katherine Hayles (b. 1947) trained in chemistry and is now the James B. Duke Professor of Literature at Duke University. Her work has explored the intersections between science and literature, and most recently digital technologies in *How We Think* (2012).

bell hooks (b. 1952) is an African-American feminist activist and scholar. Her work is an early example of intersectional analysis with a focus on race as developed in her study *Feminist Theory from Margin to Center* (1984).

Luce Irigaray (b. 1932?) is a French philosopher born in Belgium and known for her feminist critiques of philosophy, psychoanalysis, language, and structuralist linguistics. *This Sex Which Is Not One* (1985) and *Speculum of the Other Woman* (1985) are two of her many important books.

Fredric Jameson (b. 1934) is the Knut Schmidt Nielsen Professor of Comparative Literature at Duke University. He is a prolific writer and his Marxist analyses of postmodern cultural production have been very influential. They include *The Political Unconscious* (1981) and *Postmodernism, Or the Cultural Logic of Late Capitalism* (1991).

Alison Kafer is professor of feminist studies at Southwestern University, where her work focuses on the intersections of gender, sexuality, and disability as in her most recent book *Feminist, Queer, Crip* (2013).

Caren Kaplan (b. 1955) is professor of American studies at the University of California, Davis whose research interests include transnational feminism and globalization such as in her early monograph *Questions of Travel* (1996).

Katie King is Professor Emerita of women's studies at University of Maryland whose research looks at writing technologies as exemplified by her latest book, *Networked Reenactments* (2011).

Eben Kirksey is an associate professor of anthropology at Deakin University. His work focuses on multispecies ethnography as developed in his book *Emergent Ecologies* (2015).

Claude Lévi-Strauss (1908-2009) was a French anthropologist who pioneered the study of social systems and structures in works such as *The Elementary Structures of Kinship* (1967).

Sophie Lewis is a Philadelphia-based independent scholar who completed her graduate work at the University of Manchester arguing for the reconceptualization of surrogacy as labor. Her book, Full Surrogacy, is forthcoming with Verso.

Audre Lorde (1934-1992) was an African American poet, civil rights activist, essayist, and feminist famous for her protest poetry. Her works include the experimental novel *Zami* (1982) and *Sister Outsider: Essays and Speeches* (1984).

Nina Lykke (b. 1949) is a Danish feminist scholar who is professor of gender studies at Linköping University. Her work is intersectional* with a focus on gender and technology, and her publications include a co-edited volume *Between Monsters, Goddesses, and Cyborgs* (1996).

Vonda MacIntyre (b. 1948) is an award-winning US-American science fiction writer. Her works include the *Starfarers Quartet* (1989-1994). She also wrote for *Star Trek* and *Star Wars*.

Catherine MacKinnon (b. 1946) is a professor of law at the University of Michigan. Her career has focused on issues of gender equality, most influentially during the so-called feminist sex wars* of the 1970s and 1980s where she campaigned against pornography.

Herbert Marcuse (1898-1979) was a German-American Marxist philosopher. He is best known for *Eros and Civilization* (1955) and *One-Dimensional Man* (1964).

Carolyn Merchant (b. 1936) is a professor of environmental history, philosophy and ethics at the University of California, Berkeley whose work analyzes the intersection of gender, science, and the environment starting with *The Death of Nature* (1980).

Gary Olson (b. 1954) is President of Daemen College, New York. His work focuses on the theory of rhetoric and its place within literary studies.

Aiwha Ong (b. 1950) is the Robert H. Lowie Distinguished Chair in Anthropologie at the University of California, Berkeley whose interdisciplinary research most recently has focused on global technologies in *Fungible Life* (2016).

Constance Penley (b. 1948) is professor of film and media studies at the University of California, Santa Barbara whose work is situated at the intersection of film, gender and technology, such as in her early monograph *The Future of an Illusion* (1989).

Ronald Reagan (1911–2004) was a former actor who became fortieth president of the United States for two terms from 1981 to 1989.

Bernice J. Reagon (b. 1942), African-American civil rights activist who was a member of the Student Non-violent Coordinating Committee and founding member of the Albany Movement's Freedom Singers.

T. V. Reed is the Lewis E. and Stella G. Buchanan Distinguished Professor of English and American Studies at Washington State University. His research has focused on US social movements and their relation to cultural production, for example in his monograph, *Fifteen Jugglers, Five Believers* (1992).

Adrienne Rich (1929–2012) was an award-winning US-American poet, essayist, and radical feminist whose free-verse poetry explores sexuality and politics. Her works include poetry collection Diving into the *Wreck* (1973) and essay collection *Of Woman Born* (1976).

Andrew Ross (b. 1956) is professor of social and cultural analysis at New York University and closely affiliated with the journal Social Text.

Edward Said (1935-2003) was a Palestinian-American scholar whose work was central to the development of postcolonial studies. A professor in English and comparative literature at Columbia University, his most famous book was *Orientalism* (1978).

Chela Sandoval (b. 1956) is associate professor of chicana studies at the University of California, Santa Barbara whose work focuses on postcolonial feminisms, most recently in her monograph *Methodology of the Oppressed* (2000).

Malini Johar Schueller (b. 1957) is a filmmaker and professor of English at the University of Florida. Her research examines the intersections of gender, nation, and race, most recently in *US Orientalisms* (1998).

Joan W. Scott (b. 1941) is Professor Emerita in the School of Social Science at the Institute of Advanced Studies (Princeton). Her work explores the relationship between historiography and feminism, as in *Gender and the Politics of History* (1988).

Barbara Smith (b. 1946) is an African American feminist activist and writer who co-founded the Black lesbian Combahee River Collective as well as the Black press Kitchen Table.

Zoë Sofoulis is an adjunct research fellow at the Institute for Culture and Society, Western Sydney University. Her work looks at the intersection of technology, culture, and gender, for instance in her monograph *Whose Second Self?* (1993).

James Tiptree, Jr. (1915–1987) was a US-American science fiction writer and pen name of Alice B. Sheldon most noted for their short stories. Tiptree's work was preoccupied with gender and sexuality.

Hayden White (1928–2018) was a US-American historian and professor of the history of consciousness at the University of California, Santa Cruz. Key works include "The Burden of History" (1966) and *Metahistory: The Historical Imagination in Nineteenth-Century Europe* (1973).

Monique Wittig (1935–2003) was a feminist theorist and writer of fiction, born and educated in France before moving to the US in 1976. She is known for explorations of lesbian sexuality and embodiment. Important novels by her include *L'Opoponax* (1964) and *Le Corps Lesbian* (1973).

WORKS CITED

WORKS CITED

Bonner, J.T. "Review." Science 193.4252 (1976): 477–8.

Braidotti, Rosi. "A Theoretical Framework for the Critical Posthumanities." Theory, Culture & Society 0.0 (2018): 1–31.

Connery, Christopher Leigh. "Worlded Pedagogy in Santa Cruz." In The Worlding Project: Doing Cultural Studies in the Era of Globalization, edited by Rob Wilson and Christopher Leigh Connery. Santa Cruz: New Pacific Books, 2007.

Crosby, Christina. "Commentary: Allies and Enemies." In Coming to Terms: Feminism, Theory, Politics, edited by Elizabeth Weed. London: Routledge, 1989.

Doane, Mary Ann. "Commentary: Post-Utopian Difference." In Coming to Terms: Feminism, Theory, Politics, edited by Elizabeth Weed. London: Routledge, 1989.

Feigenbaum, Anna. "From cyborg feminism to drone feminism: Remembering women's anti-nuclear activisms." Feminist Theory 16.3 (2015): 265–88.

Gane, Nick, and Donna Haraway. "When We Have Never Been Human, What Is to Be Done?" Interview with Donna Haraway in Theory, Culture & Society 23 (2006): 135–58.

Halberstam, Judith (Jack). "Automating Gender: Postmodern Feminism in the Age of the Intelligent Machine." Feminist Studies 17.3 (1991): 439–60.

—. Skin Shows: Gothic Horror and the Technology of Monsters. Durham: Duke University Press, 1995.

Hayles, N. Katherine. How We Became Posthuman: Virtual Bodies in Cybernetics, Literature, and Informatics. Chicago: University of Chicago Press, 1999.

Haraway, Donna. "A Manifesto for Cyborgs: Science, Technology, and Socialist Feminism in the 1980s." Socialist Review 80 (1985): 65–107.

—. Primate Visions: Gender, Race, and Nature in the World of Modern Science. New York: Routledge, 1989.

—. The Companion Species Manifesto: Dogs, People, and Significant Otherness. Chicago: Prickly Paradigm Press, 2003.

—. When Species Meet. Minneapolis: University of Minnesota Press, 2008.

—. Staying with the Trouble: Making Kin in the Cthulucene. New York: Routledge, 2016.

Haraway, Donna, and Thyrza Goodeve. How Like a Leaf: An Interview with Donna

Haraway. New York: Routledge, 2000.

Haraway, Donna, Nina Lykke, Randi Markussen, and Finn Olesen. "Cyborgs, coyotes, and dogs: a kinship of feminist figurations" and "There are always more things going on than you thought! Methodologies as thinking technologies." In The Haraway Reader. New York: Routledge, 2004., 321–42.

Kafer, Alison. Feminist, Queer, Crip. Bloomington: Indiana University Press, 2013.

King, Katie. Networked Reenactments. Durham: Duke University Press, 2011.

Kirksey, Eben. Emergent Ecologies. Durham: Duke University Press, 2015.

Kunzru, Hari. "You Are Cyborg." Wired. February 1, 1997.

Lewis, Sophie. "Cthulhu plays no role for me." Viewpoint Magazine. May 8, 2017. https://www.viewpointmag.com/2017/05/08/cthulhu-plays-no-role-for-me/.

Lykke, Nina. Feminist Studies: A Guide to Intersectional Theory, Methodology and Writing. New York: Routledge, 2011.

MacKinnon, Catherine A. "Feminism, Marxism, Method, and the State: An Agenda for Theory." Signs 7.3 (1982): 515–44.

Olson, Gary A. "Writing, Literacy and Technology: Toward a Cyborg Writing." JAC 16.1 (1996): 1–26.

Parks, Lisa, and Caren Kaplan, eds. Life in the Age of Drone Warfare. Durham: Duke University Press, 2017.

Penley, Constance, Andrew Ross, and Donna Haraway. "Cyborgs at Large: Interview with Donna Haraway." Social Text 25-6 (1990): 8–23.

Reagon, Bernice Johnson. "Coalition Politics: Turning the Century." In Home Girls: A Black Feminist Anthology, edited by Barbara Smith. New York: Kitchen Table: Women of Color Press, 1983, 356–68.

Reed, T.V. Digitized Lives: Culture, Power, and Social Change in the Internet Era. New York: Routledge, 2014.

Sandoval, Chela. "U.S. Third World Feminism: The Theory and Method of Oppositional Consciousness in the Postmodern World." Genders 10 (1991): 1–24.

—. Methodology of the Oppressed. Minneapolis: University of Minnesota Press, 2000.

Scott, Joan W. "Commentary: Cyborgian Socialists." In Coming to Terms: Feminism, Theory, Politics, edited by Elizabeth Weed. London: Routledge, 1989.

Sofoulis, Zoë. "Cyberquake: Haraway's Manifesto." In Prefiguring Cyberculture: An Intellectual History, edited by Darren Tofts, Annemarie Jonson, and Alessio Cavallaro. Cambridge: MIT Press, 2002, 84–103.

Teich, Mikuláš. "Review." The British Journal for the History of Science 11.1 (1978): 92–4.

Wolfe, Carey. "Introduction." In Donna J. Haraway, Manifestly Haraway. Minneapolis: University of Minnesota Press, 2016.

THE MACAT LIBRARY
BY DISCIPLINE

The Macat Library By Discipline

AFRICANA STUDIES

Chinua Achebe's *An Image of Africa: Racism in Conrad's Heart of Darkness*
W. E. B. Du Bois's *The Souls of Black Folk*
Zora Neale Huston's *Characteristics of Negro Expression*
Martin Luther King Jr's *Why We Can't Wait*
Toni Morrison's *Playing in the Dark: Whiteness in the American Literary Imagination*

ANTHROPOLOGY

Arjun Appadurai's *Modernity at Large: Cultural Dimensions of Globalisation*
Philippe Ariès's *Centuries of Childhood*
Franz Boas's *Race, Language and Culture*
Kim Chan & Renée Mauborgne's *Blue Ocean Strategy*
Jared Diamond's *Guns, Germs & Steel: the Fate of Human Societies*
Jared Diamond's *Collapse: How Societies Choose to Fail or Survive*
E. E. Evans-Pritchard's *Witchcraft, Oracles and Magic Among the Azande*
James Ferguson's *The Anti-Politics Machine*
Clifford Geertz's *The Interpretation of Cultures*
David Graeber's *Debt: the First 5000 Years*
Karen Ho's *Liquidated: An Ethnography of Wall Street*
Geert Hofstede's *Culture's Consequences: Comparing Values, Behaviors, Institutes and Organizations across Nations*
Claude Lévi-Strauss's *Structural Anthropology*
Jay Macleod's *Ain't No Makin' It: Aspirations and Attainment in a Low-Income Neighborhood*
Saba Mahmood's *The Politics of Piety: The Islamic Revival and the Feminist Subjec*t
Marcel Mauss's *The Gift*

BUSINESS

Jean Lave & Etienne Wenger's *Situated Learning*
Theodore Levitt's *Marketing Myopia*
Burton G. Malkiel's *A Random Walk Down Wall Street*
Douglas McGregor's *The Human Side of Enterprise*
Michael Porter's *Competitive Strategy: Creating and Sustaining Superior Performance*
John Kotter's *Leading Change*
C. K. Prahalad & Gary Hamel's *The Core Competence of the Corporation*

CRIMINOLOGY

Michelle Alexander's *The New Jim Crow: Mass Incarceration in the Age of Colorblindness*
Michael R. Gottfredson & Travis Hirschi's *A General Theory of Crime*
Richard Herrnstein & Charles A. Murray's *The Bell Curve: Intelligence and Class Structure in American Life*
Elizabeth Loftus's *Eyewitness Testimony*
Jay Macleod's *Ain't No Makin' It: Aspirations and Attainment in a Low-Income Neighborhood*
Philip Zimbardo's *The Lucifer Effect*

ECONOMICS

Janet Abu-Lughod's *Before European Hegemony*
Ha-Joon Chang's *Kicking Away the Ladder*
David Brion Davis's *The Problem of Slavery in the Age of Revolution*
Milton Friedman's *The Role of Monetary Policy*
Milton Friedman's *Capitalism and Freedom*
David Graeber's *Debt: the First 5000 Years*
Friedrich Hayek's *The Road to Serfdom*
Karen Ho's *Liquidated: An Ethnography of Wall Street*

John Maynard Keynes's *The General Theory of Employment, Interest and Money*
Charles P. Kindleberger's *Manias, Panics and Crashes*
Robert Lucas's *Why Doesn't Capital Flow from Rich to Poor Countries?*
Burton G. Malkiel's *A Random Walk Down Wall Street*
Thomas Robert Malthus's *An Essay on the Principle of Population*
Karl Marx's *Capital*
Thomas Piketty's *Capital in the Twenty-First Century*
Amartya Sen's *Development as Freedom*
Adam Smith's *The Wealth of Nations*
Nassim Nicholas Taleb's *The Black Swan: The Impact of the Highly Improbable*
Amos Tversky's & Daniel Kahneman's *Judgment under Uncertainty: Heuristics and Biases*
Mahbub Ul Haq's *Reflections on Human Development*
Max Weber's *The Protestant Ethic and the Spirit of Capitalism*

FEMINISM AND GENDER STUDIES

Judith Butler's *Gender Trouble*
Simone De Beauvoir's *The Second Sex*
Michel Foucault's *History of Sexuality*
Betty Friedan's *The Feminine Mystique*
Saba Mahmood's *The Politics of Piety: The Islamic Revival and the Feminist Subject*
Joan Wallach Scott's *Gender and the Politics of History*
Mary Wollstonecraft's *A Vindication of the Rights of Woman*
Virginia Woolf's *A Room of One's Own*

GEOGRAPHY

The Brundtland Report's *Our Common Future*
Rachel Carson's *Silent Spring*
Charles Darwin's *On the Origin of Species*
James Ferguson's *The Anti-Politics Machine*
Jane Jacobs's *The Death and Life of Great American Cities*
James Lovelock's *Gaia: A New Look at Life on Earth*
Amartya Sen's *Development as Freedom*
Mathis Wackernagel & William Rees's *Our Ecological Footprint*

HISTORY

Janet Abu-Lughod's *Before European Hegemony*
Benedict Anderson's *Imagined Communities*
Bernard Bailyn's *The Ideological Origins of the American Revolution*
Hanna Batatu's *The Old Social Classes And The Revolutionary Movements Of Iraq*
Christopher Browning's *Ordinary Men: Reserve Police Batallion 101 and the Final Solution in Poland*
Edmund Burke's *Reflections on the Revolution in France*
William Cronon's *Nature's Metropolis: Chicago And The Great West*
Alfred W. Crosby's *The Columbian Exchange*
Hamid Dabashi's *Iran: A People Interrupted*
David Brion Davis's *The Problem of Slavery in the Age of Revolution*
Nathalie Zemon Davis's *The Return of Martin Guerre*
Jared Diamond's *Guns, Germs & Steel: the Fate of Human Societies*
Frank Dikotter's *Mao's Great Famine*
John W Dower's *War Without Mercy: Race And Power In The Pacific War*
W. E. B. Du Bois's *The Souls of Black Folk*
Richard J. Evans's *In Defence of History*
Lucien Febvre's *The Problem of Unbelief in the 16th Century*
Sheila Fitzpatrick's *Everyday Stalinism*

The Macat Library By Discipline

Eric Foner's *Reconstruction: America's Unfinished Revolution, 1863-1877*
Michel Foucault's *Discipline and Punish*
Michel Foucault's *History of Sexuality*
Francis Fukuyama's *The End of History and the Last Man*
John Lewis Gaddis's *We Now Know: Rethinking Cold War History*
Ernest Gellner's *Nations and Nationalism*
Eugene Genovese's *Roll, Jordan, Roll: The World the Slaves Made*
Carlo Ginzburg's *The Night Battles*
Daniel Goldhagen's *Hitler's Willing Executioners*
Jack Goldstone's *Revolution and Rebellion in the Early Modern World*
Antonio Gramsci's *The Prison Notebooks*
Alexander Hamilton, John Jay & James Madison's *The Federalist Papers*
Christopher Hill's *The World Turned Upside Down*
Carole Hillenbrand's *The Crusades: Islamic Perspectives*
Thomas Hobbes's *Leviathan*
Eric Hobsbawm's *The Age Of Revolution*
John A. Hobson's *Imperialism: A Study*
Albert Hourani's *History of the Arab Peoples*
Samuel P. Huntington's *The Clash of Civilizations and the Remaking of World Order*
C. L. R. James's *The Black Jacobins*
Tony Judt's *Postwar: A History of Europe Since 1945*
Ernst Kantorowicz's *The King's Two Bodies: A Study in Medieval Political Theology*
Paul Kennedy's *The Rise and Fall of the Great Powers*
Ian Kershaw's *The "Hitler Myth": Image and Reality in the Third Reich*
John Maynard Keynes's *The General Theory of Employment, Interest and Money*
Charles P. Kindleberger's *Manias, Panics and Crashes*
Martin Luther King Jr's *Why We Can't Wait*
Henry Kissinger's *World Order: Reflections on the Character of Nations and the Course of History*
Thomas Kuhn's *The Structure of Scientific Revolutions*
Georges Lefebvre's *The Coming of the French Revolution*
John Locke's *Two Treatises of Government*
Niccolò Machiavelli's *The Prince*
Thomas Robert Malthus's *An Essay on the Principle of Population*
Mahmood Mamdani's *Citizen and Subject: Contemporary Africa And The Legacy Of Late Colonialism*
Karl Marx's *Capital*
Stanley Milgram's *Obedience to Authority*
John Stuart Mill's *On Liberty*
Thomas Paine's *Common Sense*
Thomas Paine's *Rights of Man*
Geoffrey Parker's *Global Crisis: War, Climate Change and Catastrophe in the Seventeenth Century*
Jonathan Riley-Smith's *The First Crusade and the Idea of Crusading*
Jean-Jacques Rousseau's *The Social Contract*
Joan Wallach Scott's *Gender and the Politics of History*
Theda Skocpol's *States and Social Revolutions*
Adam Smith's *The Wealth of Nations*
Timothy Snyder's *Bloodlands: Europe Between Hitler and Stalin*
Sun Tzu's *The Art of War*
Keith Thomas's *Religion and the Decline of Magic*
Thucydides's *The History of the Peloponnesian War*
Frederick Jackson Turner's *The Significance of the Frontier in American History*
Odd Arne Westad's *The Global Cold War: Third World Interventions And The Making Of Our Times*

LITERATURE

Chinua Achebe's *An Image of Africa: Racism in Conrad's Heart of Darkness*
Roland Barthes's *Mythologies*
Homi K. Bhabha's *The Location of Culture*
Judith Butler's *Gender Trouble*
Simone De Beauvoir's *The Second Sex*
Ferdinand De Saussure's *Course in General Linguistics*
T. S. Eliot's *The Sacred Wood: Essays on Poetry and Criticism*
Zora Neale Huston's *Characteristics of Negro Expression*
Toni Morrison's *Playing in the Dark: Whiteness in the American Literary Imagination*
Edward Said's *Orientalism*
Gayatri Chakravorty Spivak's *Can the Subaltern Speak?*
Mary Wollstonecraft's *A Vindication of the Rights of Women*
Virginia Woolf's *A Room of One's Own*

PHILOSOPHY

Elizabeth Anscombe's *Modern Moral Philosophy*
Hannah Arendt's *The Human Condition*
Aristotle's *Metaphysics*
Aristotle's *Nicomachean Ethics*
Edmund Gettier's *Is Justified True Belief Knowledge?*
Georg Wilhelm Friedrich Hegel's *Phenomenology of Spirit*
David Hume's *Dialogues Concerning Natural Religion*
David Hume's *The Enquiry for Human Understanding*
Immanuel Kant's *Religion within the Boundaries of Mere Reason*
Immanuel Kant's *Critique of Pure Reason*
Søren Kierkegaard's *The Sickness Unto Death*
Søren Kierkegaard's *Fear and Trembling*
C. S. Lewis's *The Abolition of Man*
Alasdair MacIntyre's *After Virtue*
Marcus Aurelius's *Meditations*
Friedrich Nietzsche's *On the Genealogy of Morality*
Friedrich Nietzsche's *Beyond Good and Evil*
Plato's *Republic*
Plato's *Symposium*
Jean-Jacques Rousseau's *The Social Contract*
Gilbert Ryle's *The Concept of Mind*
Baruch Spinoza's *Ethics*
Sun Tzu's *The Art of War*
Ludwig Wittgenstein's *Philosophical Investigations*

POLITICS

Benedict Anderson's *Imagined Communities*
Aristotle's *Politics*
Bernard Bailyn's *The Ideological Origins of the American Revolution*
Edmund Burke's *Reflections on the Revolution in France*
John C. Calhoun's *A Disquisition on Government*
Ha-Joon Chang's *Kicking Away the Ladder*
Hamid Dabashi's *Iran: A People Interrupted*
Hamid Dabashi's *Theology of Discontent: The Ideological Foundation of the Islamic Revolution in Iran*
Robert Dahl's *Democracy and its Critics*
Robert Dahl's *Who Governs?*
David Brion Davis's *The Problem of Slavery in the Age of Revolution*

The Macat Library By Discipline

Alexis De Tocqueville's *Democracy in America*
James Ferguson's *The Anti-Politics Machine*
Frank Dikotter's *Mao's Great Famine*
Sheila Fitzpatrick's *Everyday Stalinism*
Eric Foner's *Reconstruction: America's Unfinished Revolution, 1863-1877*
Milton Friedman's *Capitalism and Freedom*
Francis Fukuyama's *The End of History and the Last Man*
John Lewis Gaddis's *We Now Know: Rethinking Cold War History*
Ernest Gellner's *Nations and Nationalism*
David Graeber's *Debt: the First 5000 Years*
Antonio Gramsci's *The Prison Notebooks*
Alexander Hamilton, John Jay & James Madison's *The Federalist Papers*
Friedrich Hayek's *The Road to Serfdom*
Christopher Hill's *The World Turned Upside Down*
Thomas Hobbes's *Leviathan*
John A. Hobson's *Imperialism: A Study*
Samuel P. Huntington's *The Clash of Civilizations and the Remaking of World Order*
Tony Judt's *Postwar: A History of Europe Since 1945*
David C. Kang's *China Rising: Peace, Power and Order in East Asia*
Paul Kennedy's *The Rise and Fall of Great Powers*
Robert Keohane's *After Hegemony*
Martin Luther King Jr.'s *Why We Can't Wait*
Henry Kissinger's *World Order: Reflections on the Character of Nations and the Course of History*
John Locke's *Two Treatises of Government*
Niccolò Machiavelli's *The Prince*
Thomas Robert Malthus's *An Essay on the Principle of Population*
Mahmood Mamdani's *Citizen and Subject: Contemporary Africa And The Legacy Of Late Colonialism*
Karl Marx's *Capital*
John Stuart Mill's *On Liberty*
John Stuart Mill's *Utilitarianism*
Hans Morgenthau's *Politics Among Nations*
Thomas Paine's *Common Sense*
Thomas Paine's *Rights of Man*
Thomas Piketty's *Capital in the Twenty-First Century*
Robert D. Putman's *Bowling Alone*
John Rawls's *Theory of Justice*
Jean-Jacques Rousseau's *The Social Contract*
Theda Skocpol's *States and Social Revolutions*
Adam Smith's *The Wealth of Nations*
Sun Tzu's *The Art of War*
Henry David Thoreau's *Civil Disobedience*
Thucydides's *The History of the Peloponnesian War*
Kenneth Waltz's *Theory of International Politics*
Max Weber's *Politics as a Vocation*
Odd Arne Westad's *The Global Cold War: Third World Interventions And The Making Of Our Times*

POSTCOLONIAL STUDIES

Roland Barthes's *Mythologies*
Frantz Fanon's *Black Skin, White Masks*
Homi K. Bhabha's *The Location of Culture*
Gustavo Gutiérrez's *A Theology of Liberation*
Edward Said's *Orientalism*
Gayatri Chakravorty Spivak's *Can the Subaltern Speak?*

PSYCHOLOGY

Gordon Allport's *The Nature of Prejudice*
Alan Baddeley & Graham Hitch's *Aggression: A Social Learning Analysis*
Albert Bandura's *Aggression: A Social Learning Analysis*
Leon Festinger's *A Theory of Cognitive Dissonance*
Sigmund Freud's *The Interpretation of Dreams*
Betty Friedan's *The Feminine Mystique*
Michael R. Gottfredson & Travis Hirschi's *A General Theory of Crime*
Eric Hoffer's *The True Believer: Thoughts on the Nature of Mass Movements*
William James's *Principles of Psychology*
Elizabeth Loftus's *Eyewitness Testimony*
A. H. Maslow's *A Theory of Human Motivation*
Stanley Milgram's *Obedience to Authority*
Steven Pinker's *The Better Angels of Our Nature*
Oliver Sacks's *The Man Who Mistook His Wife For a Hat*
Richard Thaler & Cass Sunstein's *Nudge: Improving Decisions About Health, Wealth and Happiness*
Amos Tversky's *Judgment under Uncertainty: Heuristics and Biases*
Philip Zimbardo's *The Lucifer Effect*

SCIENCE

Rachel Carson's *Silent Spring*
William Cronon's *Nature's Metropolis: Chicago And The Great West*
Alfred W. Crosby's *The Columbian Exchange*
Charles Darwin's *On the Origin of Species*
Richard Dawkin's *The Selfish Gene*
Thomas Kuhn's *The Structure of Scientific Revolutions*
Geoffrey Parker's *Global Crisis: War, Climate Change and Catastrophe in the Seventeenth Century*
Mathis Wackernagel & William Rees's *Our Ecological Footprint*

SOCIOLOGY

Michelle Alexander's *The New Jim Crow: Mass Incarceration in the Age of Colorblindness*
Gordon Allport's *The Nature of Prejudice*
Albert Bandura's *Aggression: A Social Learning Analysis*
Hanna Batatu's *The Old Social Classes And The Revolutionary Movements Of Iraq*
Ha-Joon Chang's *Kicking Away the Ladder*
W. E. B. Du Bois's *The Souls of Black Folk*
Émile Durkheim's *On Suicide*
Frantz Fanon's *Black Skin, White Masks*
Frantz Fanon's *The Wretched of the Earth*
Eric Foner's *Reconstruction: America's Unfinished Revolution, 1863-1877*
Eugene Genovese's *Roll, Jordan, Roll: The World the Slaves Made*
Jack Goldstone's *Revolution and Rebellion in the Early Modern World*
Antonio Gramsci's *The Prison Notebooks*
Richard Herrnstein & Charles A Murray's *The Bell Curve: Intelligence and Class Structure in American Life*
Eric Hoffer's *The True Believer: Thoughts on the Nature of Mass Movements*
Jane Jacobs's *The Death and Life of Great American Cities*
Robert Lucas's *Why Doesn't Capital Flow from Rich to Poor Countries?*
Jay Macleod's *Ain't No Makin' It: Aspirations and Attainment in a Low Income Neighborhood*
Elaine May's *Homeward Bound: American Families in the Cold War Era*
Douglas McGregor's *The Human Side of Enterprise*
C. Wright Mills's *The Sociological Imagination*

The Macat Library By Discipline

Thomas Piketty's *Capital in the Twenty-First Century*
Robert D. Putman's *Bowling Alone*
David Riesman's *The Lonely Crowd: A Study of the Changing American Character*
Edward Said's *Orientalism*
Joan Wallach Scott's *Gender and the Politics of History*
Theda Skocpol's *States and Social Revolutions*
Max Weber's *The Protestant Ethic and the Spirit of Capitalism*

THEOLOGY

Augustine's *Confessions*
Benedict's *Rule of St Benedict*
Gustavo Gutiérrez's *A Theology of Liberation*
Carole Hillenbrand's *The Crusades: Islamic Perspectives*
David Hume's *Dialogues Concerning Natural Religion*
Immanuel Kant's *Religion within the Boundaries of Mere Reason*
Ernst Kantorowicz's *The King's Two Bodies: A Study in Medieval Political Theology*
Søren Kierkegaard's *The Sickness Unto Death*
C. S. Lewis's *The Abolition of Man*
Saba Mahmood's *The Politics of Piety: The Islamic Revival and the Feminist Subjec*t
Baruch Spinoza's *Ethics*
Keith Thomas's *Religion and the Decline of Magic*

Printed in the United States
by Baker & Taylor Publisher Services